OMNIVORE-TESTED, VEGAN

Calling all omnivores!! Have you always wanted to try a plant-based diet but didn't know where to begin? Do you have a vegan friend or loved one you'd like to cook for but don't know how? Are you just looking for recipes to use occasionally that don't include animal products? *Winner Winner Vegan Dinner* has the answers you've been looking for! Pleasing the palate of omnivores and vegans alike, *Winner Winner Vegan Dinner* includes recipes such as:

> Sloppy Joe's Cousin with Syracuse Salt Potatoes
> Roasted Veggie Sandwiches with Pesto Aioli
> Italian Sausage Soup
> Jaclyn's Jambalaya
> All-Star Ice Cream Fudge
> AND MANY MORE!!!

"I didn't realize the words *delicious* and *vegan* belong in the same sentence, but your book proves they do. Your recipes show that you don't have to be a vegan to enjoy eating like one!"
- Emily Schwartz, founder of www.TheTimeDiet.org

"My family and I are not vegans. We aren't vegetarians either. However, after trying a few of Jaclyn's recipes, my life has changed. And being the person who mainly cooks for our family of seven, it has changed the way my family eats. I used to feel that every meal had to have some kind of meat as the main dish. Now I know that I have options. We all actually prefer most of our meals to be vegetarian now! I am grateful that Jaclyn has shown us through her amazing recipes that eating a healthier diet free from animal products can be yummy and satisfying. I will be telling everyone I know about her recipe book!"
- Chelsea J.

"You don't have to be vegan to appreciate these delicious, nutritious, easy-to-make recipes. Jaclyn has convinced me to incorporate more plant-based recipes into my family's diet!"
-Sheree L.

"An adventurous spirit is behind this great cookbook. For five years I have been a delighted taste tester for Jaclyn's recipes. Since I have not convinced her to move in as my personal chef, this tried and tested volume of her recipes will do just fine. It is a practical cookbook that guides an omnivore towards a plant-based diet in small doses. *Winner Winner Vegan Dinner* is highly recommended for anyone desiring a healthier lifestyle."
-Jean L.

Winner Winner Vegan Dinner

Bridging the Gap Between Dietary Worlds

Jaclyn Quamo

Foreword by Thomas Lodi, MD, MD(H), CNS

Dedicated to Nonnie,

My culinary inspiration and
a true genius in the kitchen.

Foreword

I am honored to know Jaclyn and Jeff Quamo. Their purity of heart and love of truth are rare blessings in today's world. Even when one is seemingly prepared to hear and live the truth, it is quite a formidable undertaking that cannot be approached with anything less than an impassioned devotion and an earnest heart. The temptations regarding the foods we eat are far greater and more insidious than that of any other temptations that plague the flesh.

This is true, not only because we all NEED to eat, but, moreover, by the time we are three years of age, our appetites have been formed. The veracity of that last statement is clear when one considers the ease with which a two year old can be persuaded to eat something new but try that with a four year old.

And, as if that weren't enough, we have been inundated with myths and false claims regarding diet and health, mostly by commercial interests but even by others who actually believe the pseudo-academics they profess.

One of the most powerful of all these myths, one which is responsible for more deaths than all the wars of the twentieth century, is ***the protein myth***. The angelic and pristine minds of our children sit as helpless prey to the vultures of commerce as they turn over not only their minds but also their innocence to the producers and financiers of television entertainment.

These myths and mistruths have so permeated our culture that they have become constituent to all curricula and are now considered to be a priori knowledge, that is, they are thought to be self- evident. And then, accordingly, these untruths have become integral to our most sacred institutions from schools to churches and from sports to business to government.

"If you repeat a lie enough, it becomes the truth" is a concept that arose out of the Nazi propaganda machine.

That we are omnivores by perversion and not by design is clear to anyone who has sought in earnest to understand the subject. All true omnivores must be anatomically capable of killing their prey when there are no suitable plants available. Killing must be practical and efficient and, in that regard, all mammalian omnivores have snouts and pointed claws to rend, kill and devour their victims just as proficiently as carnivores.

Bears, raccoons, skunks and rats are among this group wherein it can be seen that they possess much of killing apparatus of carnivores, such as sharp teeth with elongated cupids (eye teeth), no cheeks to get in the way of delivering a death bite to the neck and large, sharp claws for shredding the flesh into bite size pieces. What is not outwardly visible are the adaptations these creatures have in their intestinal anatomy allowing them to digest and assimilate large volumes of plant material. These are all true omnivores.

Clearly, humans are neither adapted to killing animals without the use of tools (weapons) nor instinctively driven to eat them. We do not look upon a cow grazing in the field and lick our lips while salivating. Lions do! Neither do we come upon the corpse of an animal and begin to sniff the remains carefully while salivating. Hyenas do! As a matter of fact, we find that our usual practice is to disguise the decayed flesh which has found its way to our dinner plates to such an extent that it no longer resembles the corpse from which it was removed.

In large part, it is actually the sauces and gravies that enslave our palates, not the actual flesh itself. The butter, garlic and lemon used to sauté mushrooms are the same as are used to prepare escargot (snails). If the snails were simply placed on a plate without any preparation, this delicacy, I might add, would lose its savor and favor. Consider, though, that when mushrooms are sautéed in this same delicate sauce, not only are the aroma and taste preserved but also the texture of the snail remains for the epicurean who has decided to eat with a bit more wisdom while satisfying his perverted tastes. Likewise, unless it were broiled and prepared with a particular culinary artistry to earn it the designation as filet mignon, an extracted muscle from either side of the spine taken from the carcass of a steer would have very few takers. The old American standard, the hamburger, is simply ground up muscles, organs, brain and spinal tissue and yet it is renowned worldwide to both delight and addict people by the billions.   What then can account for its distinction and acclaim?   Certainly not the usual body parts. No, it is the mixture and preparation of sauces and spices that have been empirically tested on billions over the decades that account for its almost immediate acceptance into every culture to which it is exported.

Flesh eating is so antithetical to our very natures that we not only must camouflage the sight, smell and taste of the animal parts we consume, we must also assign them different names, such as hotdogs, chops, nuggets, etc. Hence, rather than offering our loved ones pig corpse and chicken embryos for breakfast, we entice them with words like bacon & eggs.

Proteins, carbohydrates and fats constitute the macronutrients required for life, while micronutrients are composed of vitamins and minerals. That proteins are necessary for structure and function is not the question, but rather from what source and what quantity are proteins compatible with health?

Anyone who has witnessed a helpless, newborn baby drink luxuriously from its mother's breast and, over nine to twelve months, double in weight and size can attest to the fact that there is ample protein available for humans in human milk. The percentage of calories derived from protein in human milk is the lowest of all mammalian milk. Whereas rats' milk is approximately 49% protein, cats' milk approximately 32% protein and chimpanzees' milk approximately 7% protein, human milk only contains from 3 to 5% of calories from protein. This then is the amount of protein ordained by Nature (God) to be necessary and sufficient for humans during that period of life when their growth rate is at a maximum. Teenagers, who grow at a fairly rapid rate, don't even double their size. They don't grow from four feet to eight feet in height.

As can be seen by the following partial list, it is quite difficult NOT to get adequate protein from vegetables. In other words, the reason that you prefer to eat grass fed cows is due to the fact that both the size and health of their muscles (meat) is far superior to those poor creatures forced to feed on other cows, road kill and euthanized pets as is common in modern farming and agribusiness.

- *SPINACH = 49%*
- *BROCCOLI = 45%*
- *CAULIFLOWER = 40%*
- *LETTUCE = 34%*
- *PEAS = 30%*
- *GREEN BEANS = 26%*
- *CUCUMBERS = 24%*
- *CELERY = 21%*
- *POTATOES = 11%*

Next time you see a horse, ask him, "Where do you get your protein?" Even a peach contains 6% protein and a banana 5% protein by calorie.

"If a little is great and a lot is better, then way too much is just about right!" This quote by Mae West from the early part of the twentieth century pretty much sums up the American attitude about most things, which is why we Americans consume the majority of the world's resources. This, however, turns out to be true of absolutely nothing. Too much oxygen and we develop emphysema, too much water and our blood becomes diluted to the point of not being capable of sustaining life. When the protein content of our diets averages around 5%, we are able to meet all of our protein requirements. Once our protein intake exceeds 10%, we develop chronic, degenerative conditions known as diseases. And once we exceed 20%, cancer can be expected.

So, "we need what we need in the amount that we need, nothing more and nothing less" would be a wiser aphorism by which to live.

If we are to remain successfully unentangled by our ferocious appetites, hearing and/or reading about these truths must become part of our daily lives. However, even daily reading and fruitful discussions with friends regarding these truths is still not enough.

The power of appetite should never be underestimated.

Witness the smoker, the alcoholic, the drug addict and the morbidly obese. All of them know in their hearts that they should stop and, in fact, shed many a tear on their way to procure their addictive substances. What this book will allow you to do is satisfy your appetites while preserving your health. Remember, the price of indulging does not need to be your health!

Thomas Lodi, MD, MD(H), CNS
Bangkok, Thailand
July 29, 2013

Contents

Breakfast   Winner

Quick and Simple Meals

		Winner
Sweet Dill Carrots	71	☐
Saucy Chicks	72	☐
Jaclyn's Jambalaya	73	☐

Going with the Grain

Cuban Rice	75	☐
Savory Quinoa	76	☐
Lemon Paprika Rice	77	☐
Quinoa and Bean Chili	78	☐
Spanish-Style Rice	79	☐
Scrappy Meal #2	80	☐

For Soup Lovers

Cream of Broccoli Soup	82	☐
Simply Succotash	83	☐
Italian Wedding Soup	84	☐
We Three Lentils Stew	85	☐
Peruvian Purple Soup	86	☐
Salsa Soup	87	☐
Scrappy Meal #3	88	☐
Momma's Dumpling Soup	89	☐
Italian Sausage Soup	90	☐
Whole Wheat Irish Soda Bread	91	☐
Sweet Cornbread	92	☐

Sweet Tooths Anonymous

Cookie Truffles	94	☐
All-Star Ice Cream Fudge	95	☐
Mango Raspberry Sorbet	96	☐

Party Time

Fresh Juice

Resources I Rely On and Recommend

Index

"Everyone has a doctor in him or her; we just have to help it in its work. The natural healing force within each one of us is the greatest force in getting well. Our food should be our medicine. Our medicine should be our food."   -Hippocrates

Acknowledgements

To LaDonna Welsh: Thank you for being you! She is the sole inspiration for this book. She was once a coworker and is someone I have always looked up to. After several discussions about nutrition in the teachers' lounge, she decided that she wanted to become vegan. She quickly realized what a change it was and expressed some frustration. This reminded me of when I first started and of how frustrated and lost I felt when I turned my back on my former eating habits. I wouldn't wish that upon anyone who wants to switch to a plant-based diet. One afternoon it just hit me that I needed to compile a recipe book to bridge the gap and ease the transition between dietary worlds. My goal is that you will enjoy tasting these new recipes and that you will experience less frustration in adapting to a new way of eating. If you choose not to switch but to occasionally enjoy a plant-based meal, I hope that this book will help you.

To Dr. Thomas Lodi: It is easy to say that you have changed my life forever. I will always feel indebted to you for your friendship, your willingness to help and your passionate desire to educate others about eating habits. Thank you for all you do.

To Linda Shaw: Thank you for sharing your talents in editing my book. I treasure our friendship and I am honored that you have become a part of this journey with me.

To Emily Schwartz: Thank you for sharing your knowledge and experiences with the self-publishing world. I could not have done this without you.

To my taste and recipe testers: It is impossible to name all of you as I was bold enough to ask complete strangers to taste some samples. I would like to thank those who were my consistently brave taste testers during the past eighteen months; they are the wonderfully amazing staff members at Irving Elementary and the following individuals and their families: Maya Lopez, Erryn Parr and Natasha Monahan. Many thanks also go to the following individuals, my culinary heroes, who were my valiant recipe testers; their time and honesty has been greatly appreciated: Allison Allen, Lynn Allred, Alyson Ancheta, Lauren Besich, Bridget Biggs, Christine Bradley, Amarilis Brewer, Lisanne Brooks, Meilyn Bushman, Nancy Campbell, Carol Cherry, Melanie Clark, Elyse Coleman, Alicia Comerford, Alice DeWitt, Stephanie Dutro, Krysten Glor, Crystal Gorishek, Olga Grant, Jolene Herman, Mat Herrmann, Melissa Herrmann, Jen Hilliard, Dawn Holloman, Eva Johnston, Chelsea Jones, Monica Keeton, Ruth Landeros, Molly Letcher, Sheree Liddiard, Natasha Monahan, Tiffany Mortensen, Eileen Nichols, Nicole Pablo, Alana Parker, Emily Park-Friend, Erryn Parr, Alli

Putnam, Pam Quamo, Christy Shaw, Linda Shaw, Sarah Steele, Natasha Thackeray, Jessica Trueman, Meredith Vaughn Hey, Terrie Villalba and Wendy Yates.

To my most cherished friend and original omnivore taste taster, Jean Luce: Words cannot express how much your friendship has both blessed and enriched my life. I look forward to many more years of Jaclyn and Jean adventures!

To my parents: I am indebted to you for all that you've sacrificed and taught me, for the awesome memories and the love you have had for each other and for me and my sisters. When I became a wife and a mother myself, I had your examples to rely on. Thank you from the bottom of my heart. I love you both!

To my sisters: I am so happy that we have shared our lives together. I am in awe of your talents and willingness to serve others. Thank you for always being willing to try my food and for being the amazing women that you are. The world is truly a better place because you are both a part of it!

To my cousin Travis: Although we don't see each other or talk often, when we do, I truly value every second. Thank you for your encouragement and the late night laughs that have left me in tears. You are awesome!

To my in-laws: Thank you for welcoming me into your family, for supporting our marriage and for the love and laughs we share together. I am honored to be a Quamo and hope to represent the name well.

To my husband: What can I say? You are my *favorite* boy! I cannot believe that I am so blessed as to be your wife and the mother of your kids. You are my mentor, my rock, my best friend and the keeper of my heart forever. Thank you for your love and support, for the comic relief and for choosing to share your life with me. You are truly a saint for eating all of the food I've made you taste test over and over again. I cherish you for whom you are and always thank Heavenly Father that you are in my life. Here's to an eternity of crazy adventures! I can't think of a better person to share them with.

To my little one: Your laugh, smile, sense of humor and love have melted my heart time and time again. I am so grateful that Heavenly Father has entrusted us to be your parents. I am honored to be your mother and to watch you grow up to become the individual He needs you to be.

Last, but not least, I wish to thank my Heavenly Father: I thank Thee for sharing Thy wisdom, guidance and love throughout my life and during this writing process. Despite the fact that I feel deeply inadequate as a recipe book author, I have total faith in following this prompting from Thee. With God, all things truly ARE possible! I look forward to the day when I can embrace Thee and Thy Son again. I hope to always have the courage to do the things Thou would have me do. Till we meet again!

Introduction

As I have thought about my life, I think that I was always meant to be a vegan. While growing up, I was always the lucky one to find bones in processed meat products. Whether it was chicken nuggets, chicken patties, hamburgers, hot dogs, or veal patties, you name it, more than once I found a bone. I reacted by feeling sick to my stomach and losing my appetite.

After living in Arizona for about a year, my husband Jeff and I started a private studio for clarinet students. Through the studio we have gotten to know some great kids and their equally great families. One family, in particular, changed our lives forever. Week after week my husband came home late from lessons at the studio. Sometimes he was two hours late. It drove me nuts! When I finally asked him about it, Jeff invited me to come at the end of his last student's lesson. It was there that I met that student's father, Dr. Thomas Lodi, the founder of *An Oasis of Healing*. He spoke to my husband for an hour or two after each lesson and shared his vast knowledge of health and nutrition and his successful methods for bringing patients back to health from illnesses as serious as stage IV cancer *without* the use of surgeries, radiation or traditional chemotherapy. His blunt, unapologetic approach to explaining health through nutrition left us in a daze. He recommended that we read *The China Study* by T. Colin Campbell. We quickly bought the book. When we were halfway through it, we completely gave up meat and milk. We were taken aback at what we were learning which was completely opposite from what we had been taught. Jeff was the one who wanted to begin adopting these recommendations, and, out of laziness, not wanting to make two different meals each night, I decided to join him. It took us a year to wean ourselves off of all dairy products, especially cheese. But do it, we did, and we have felt great ever since. We will be forever grateful to Dr. Lodi for sharing his knowledge and experiences with us.

An immediate benefit which my husband noticed was that he lost twenty five pounds, without even trying, in the first six weeks. Throughout his life he had had at least six sinus infections a year. Since we became vegan, he has not even had one in six years.

The biggest benefit for me is that my digestive system has been much happier. My family affectionately joked about my irritable stomach. I can't tell you the number of times that my parents had to pull over on the side of the road during a trip because of my upset stomach or the times I had to dash to the bathroom after a few bites of a meal. My worst moment occurred while hiking up a mountain in Arizona. My husband and I were a mile up with a quarter of a mile left to go when I realized that a pyroclastic flow urgently needed to erupt from my backside. There I was with nowhere to hide in the barren desert landscaping. In a total panic I spun around in circles several times while trying to assess my situation. What was I to do? We were on a day hike, I had no toilet paper and there were no tree leaves anywhere. What could I do? I asked for my husband's t-shirt and I'll let you imagine the rest. True love is when your spouse still drives you home after you've conducted an anal exorcism on a mountainside.

Why There is a Need for this Book

To bridge the gap between dietary worlds: When we made the switch to eating a plant-based diet, it was overwhelming, hard and stressful. Despite the dozen or so vegan recipe books which I'd purchased, I had more failures than successes. Talk about frustration! When I was an omnivore, I always looked forward to making my menu and grocery list for the week. That all changed when I spent two hours each week in tears surrounded by recipe books without knowing what to choose. After many years of trial and error, I love making my grocery lists again. This book is for anyone who is willing to eat a plant-based diet but has been afraid to start. These recipes mostly use ingredients that aren't too unusual. In order to enhance the probability of success, these recipes have been both taste tested and recipe tested by omnivores. Yes, that's right, omnivores. I did this because, in my mind, if omnivores enjoy these vegan recipes, then they must be good and will make your transition easier.

To assist omnivores with caring hearts: Many of my omnivore family members and friends have wanted to invite us over for a meal or to give us a holiday treat, but they don't know what to prepare. I think that this is a common occurrence. Omnivores want to prepare meals for vegetarians and vegans but don't know where to find winning recipes. Well, look no further! My hope is that the omnivores of the world will feel confident in the kitchen when preparing these plant-based meals for their friends and loved ones and will also enjoy eating the food.

To expand the omnivore's palate: Many omnivores have no interest in solely eating a plant-based diet. What we put into our bodies is a choice that we each are entitled to make and I respect that.

Many of the omnivores that I know do have a desire for an occasional plant-based meal. Enjoy these recipes! No matter how many plant-based meals you decide to consume each week, I hope that you will find joy in the journey using these recipes.

To assist those following the Word of Wisdom: Those of my faith are very familiar with Section 89 of the Doctrine and Covenants. For more focus, verses 12-13 state the following: "Yea, flesh also of beasts and of the fowls of the air, I, the Lord, have ordained for the use of man with thanksgiving; nevertheless they are to be used *sparingly*; And it is *pleasing* unto me that they *should not be used*, only in times of winter, or of cold, or famine (emphasis added)." What does this mean for you and your family? That is between you and Heavenly Father. Many members I've spoken with have come to me wanting meatless meal ideas, so here they are!

Before We Get Started

Using this book: This book enables you to keep track of which recipes you have tried. I drive myself nuts when preparing a new recipe only to realize halfway through that I've already made it. Even worse yet, I didn't like it the first time. Each recipe page has a place to write in the date you tried it as well as whether or not you think it's a winner. At the bottom of the page you will find some space in case you make any changes so that you can remember them the next time you make it. After trying each recipe, go to the "Contents" page where you will find a place to check mark the recipe as a winner or to mark an X if it is not. This will be a quick and easy way to glance through the recipes and pick a new one or to return to one you like. Those who own an electronic version of this book may want to keep a journal to keep track of which recipes that have been tried and how you judged them.

Can't find the exact ingredients: I only mention specific brand names because of personal preference. There are several great brands from which to choose. Experiment and decide which you like best. If you can't find what you want, look on-line for the resources in your area, talk to a vegan friend or ask if your grocer could start carrying those items.

Cooked beans: After cooking beans, I like to put 1 ½ cups portions, drained, into quart-sized re-sealable plastic freezer bags, then lay them flat in the freezer. I try to use them within a month. When I need a 15 ounce can of beans, I simply submerge one freezer bag of beans in a large bowl of hot water. Freezing the beans flat reduces the thawing time as there is more surface area exposed to hot water.

Dry legumes, i.e., lentils and beans: Be sure to search through your legumes as you may occasionally find small pebbles; pull them out and rinse the legumes with water to remove any dirt.

Evaporated cane juice: This is an unrefined sugar. It looks like regular sugar granules; it is light brown in color. We use Wholesome® Sweeteners Organic Sugar which, if you check the ingredients, is just organic evaporated cane juice.

Green chiles: I buy large jars of prepared green chiles from my local bulk store. Just so you know, if you can only find canned, one 4 ounce can of diced green chiles equals about a ¼ cup portion.

Ground flax seeds: I buy whole flax seeds and then use my coffee grinder to pulverize them into a powder-like consistency.

Melon baller madness: When making fresh juices I use a melon baller to remove the seeds from apples and pears, thus minimizing waste. Simply cut the apple or pear in half length-wise and then use the melon baller to scoop out the seeds. When I made this discovery, I did a huge happy dance.

Non-dairy milk: This is milk that does not come from an animal. Luckily, in our day and age there are several non-dairy milk options. Here are just a few of the many: almond milk, coconut milk, flax milk, hemp milk, oat milk, rice milk and soy milk.

Organic food: There is a debate about whether or not organic foods are more nutritious. Decide for yourself! In my experience, besides the fact that you won't have harmful chemicals on or in your food, organic tastes better! After years of eating organic foods, it isn't easy to eat non-organic; the taste of non-organic just doesn't measure up to the organic standard that I have become accustomed to eating. Whenever I have a choice, I buy organic. Some people choose to pay the equivalent of a mortgage payment for a handbag, as for me, I like spending a few extra dollars at the grocery store.

Plant-based wax paper: The regular waxed papers on the market are made with beeswax or animal fat, a vegan no-no. I like to use If You Care® All Natural Waxed Paper which is made from soybeans. If you are making a recipe requiring waxed paper and cannot find it yourself, ask your vegan guests beforehand if they have some waxed paper you can use. Chances are that they will be tickled pink that you are being so accommodating.

Semi-sweet vegan chocolate chips: We like to use Enjoy Life® Semi-Sweet Chocolate Mini Chips.

Using whole wheat flour and brown rice: If you are not accustomed to using these, then it may take an adjustment. Foods made with whole wheat flour are heavier and denser than those you may be used to. Same goes with brown rice versus white rice. Brown rice has a different taste which we really love; with time, you will, too.

Vegan vegetable broth: I love, love, love Rapunzel Vegan Vegetable Bouillon with Sea Salt. Enough said. Please note on the package that 1 cube equals 2 cups of broth.

White bean puree: Take one 15 ounce can of white beans, drain, rinse and puree with ¼ cup of water in a food processor. This makes approximately 1 cup of white bean puree. Whatever I don't use, I freeze in ice cube trays covered with plastic wrap. Once frozen, I pop them in a quart-sized re-sealable plastic freezer bag and return to the freezer for later use. One cube equals approximately a $\frac{1}{8}$ cup portion. So here is the simple math: 2 cubes = ¼ cup, 4 cubes = ½ cup, 8 cubes = 1 cup. Simply thaw the cubes when needed.

Frequently Asked Questions

1.) What are some of the physical benefits one may experience when eating a vegan diet?
Because of bio-chemical individuality, the areas of improvement vary from person to person. This list is not all-inclusive:

Blood sugar levels
Blood pressure, circulation
Body mass index
Bone density
Bowel regularity
Brain health: memory, clarity, concentration
Dental health, fresher breath
Energy
Fertility
Hair, nails, skin

Immunity
Menstrual cycle
Mental health
Senses of smell and taste
Sex drive
Sleep patterns
Weight loss
Well-being, youthful look
Workouts better, faster recovery

Expect fewer of these and other problems:

Abdominal discomfort
Addictions, cravings
Allergies, urticaria
Anemia
Anxiety, depression
Arthritis, gout
Body odor
Cancer
Canker sores
Cholesterol problems
Dental problems

Digestive difficulties
Dysmenorrhea
Elimination issues
Headaches
Heart irregularities
Infections
Respiratory challenges
Skin problems
Snoring
Varicose veins
Weight struggles

As a bonus, here are some of the non-physical benefits to eating vegan:

Animal awareness
Cooking: love for, increased skills
Desire to learn and change
Environmental concerns
Influence peers, sensitivity to others
Motivation
Palate expands
Relaxation
Self-assurance, self-worth
Spirituality

2.) What can and can't vegans eat?

Vegans can eat anything from plant-based sources, preferably, in my humble opinion, organic. Anything that comes from an animal is off limits. When buying something at the store, ask yourself if this comes from an animal or a plant. Reading ingredient labels for packaged items is a must. Sorry, folks, but it's the truth. Regardless of whether or not an ingredient is plant-based, if you can't pronounce it, avoid it. Reading the ingredients is very revealing. Now when I read the ingredients of the products I used to eat, I am shocked and disgusted at what I've found. Read the ingredient labels, period. Luckily, more and more products are being clearly labeled as vegan. Ask many questions at restaurants. A few questions which I ask when eating at a new place are: 'Is there lard in your beans or chips?' 'Is there dairy (butter, cream, milk, cheese, yogurt etc.) in that?' 'Is there fish oil in your curry?'

3.) What impact does a vegan diet have on the world?

Read *The Food Revolution: How Your Diet Can Help Save Your Life And Our World* by John Robbins. Even as a seasoned vegan, my jaw often dropped while reading this book.

4.) Don't you miss _____? How do you get over your cravings for _____?

A lot of people say that they couldn't go vegan because they would miss XYZ too much. Let me tell you that since going vegan, my tastes have changed drastically. Food addictions are no more; the cravings are gone. I don't crave or miss cheese, once my favorite snack. I don't miss juicy hamburgers. And yes, not even pepperoni pizza! I've been off the Standard American Diet (SAD) for so long that I honestly have no desire to go back.

5.) Is the transition to a vegan diet difficult?

Here's the low down:

Physically, some people go through a detox period while their bodies are flushing out a lifetime accumulation of toxins and junk. Each person experiences it differently. Some feel like they have the flu, some have diarrhea, some get headaches and others feel no different at all. I didn't really have any symptoms, but my husband, on the other hand, had to stay within ten feet of the bathroom for about ten days. He had eaten chicken and refined pasta every day, so his body had to adjust. After those ten days, he felt like a new person.

Psychologically, it may be a challenge at first. You may have lingering cravings in the very beginning. When we first gave up meat, I hadn't completely cleaned out our fridge and pantry. It was about day two when I saw a package of pepperoni slices in my fridge. I ate a handful, forgave myself, and threw out the rest. It's not all or nothing, especially in the beginning. The more you learn about the benefits of a plant-based diet, the more motivated you will feel to stick with it. After a few weeks without meat, my school cafeteria was serving spaghetti with meat sauce, one of my favorites. My logic told me to scrape off the meat and enjoy the lunch. WRONG! Even after those few short weeks, my body did not like the reintroduction of meat and I had stabbing pains in my stomach for the rest of that afternoon. It was then that I knew that there was no turning back for me.

Emotionally, you need to be prepared for a little added stress when eating with others. Here are some things that have helped us along the way:

> a.) Eat beforehand. If you know that you are going to a party where there are no options for you, eat before going to minimize the temptation to eat foods you shouldn't. I always attend church gatherings and parties where dinner is served. I eat before and then snack on veggies or whatever there is and socialize with those around me. After all, the company is the main reason we gather together, right?

b.) Offer to bring a dish to share. There is nothing wrong with bringing a dish for you to eat as well as for others to enjoy.

c.) Offer to have dinner at your house. Prepare a favorite vegan meal which you think others will enjoy.

d.) Suggest a restaurant with vegan options. As you do more research and ask more questions, you will find that several restaurants, including chain restaurants, have vegan options. I will often look up a menu online ahead of time. When at a new restaurant, I'm not afraid to ask questions. Being extremely polite and giving many sincere compliments throughout the meal to the server helps everyone to have a good experience. While there may be some extra planning, it is definitely worth it.

6.) Where do you get your protein?

There are so many great plant-based sources of protein that it is impossible to list them all. Here are some of our favorites:

Broccoli; brown rice; dark leafy greens, i.e., kale, spinach; Field Roast® Sausages; legumes; nuts and nut butters; seeds, i.e., flax, pumpkin, sunflower; whole grains, i.e., quinoa, whole wheat and whole grain pastas.

7.) Where do you get your calcium?

Again, there are many sources. Here are our favorites:

Almonds; blackstrap molasses; broccoli; chia seeds; coconut milk and coconut milk yogurt; dark leafy greens, i.e., collards, kale, spinach; figs; legumes; oranges; sesame seeds and sunflower seeds.

8.) How much time do you spend making dinner each night?

That depends. Sometimes I spend thirty to forty minutes while other nights less than fifteen. Recipes that require baking take longer, but you can just set your kitchen timer and accomplish whatever else you need to do. If you won't be at home for very long, check out the recipes in the "Quick and Simple Meals" section as most only take about fifteen minutes to fix. Pita pizza nights have saved me several times when running from work to the babysitter, home and then to a rehearsal. I have gotten faster and more efficient at chopping vegetables. If your weeknights are super busy, chop all of your vegetables over the weekend and store them in containers in the refrigerator until you need them.

9.) How much do you spend a week on groceries?

Although we budget $200 a week, we usually spend less than that. Keep in mind that this also includes juicing at least five times a week. If I stick to my grocery list, I may spend $120 to $150. Some weeks I spend as little as $90, while others I exceed $200. Why the big range in spending? When I see sales at the grocery stores and use my coupons, I stock up. I love saving money whenever I can.

10.) Where do you shop?

I am a Whole Foods® Market junkie. I love them. Their produce is amazing. The workers are fantastic and whenever I've had to return an item, they don't bat an eyelash. When we take road trips, especially cross-country, we plan our stops based on where they are located. I know that maybe I'm a little obsessive, but, hey, when you are in love with something, you're in love. When we are in our home town in New York where there isn't a Whole Foods® Market, Wegmans® is our favorite place to shop. I also love to shop at Sprouts®. There are many awesome grocery stores out there. It depends on your area. Do your own research and find grocery stores that provide plant-based options. Sometimes your local grocery store may be able to carry a product you are looking for. There is no harm in asking politely. Also, don't underestimate the value of your local farmers' market!

11.) These portions are very large, some feeding double what is listed. Why is that?

I have a little confession. Our family eats large portions. My coworkers can't believe how much I eat at lunch, sometimes twice as much as they do. It's been like that my whole life. Freeze some of the leftovers for another meal or plan to eat them for lunch the next day. Even better, when you are making some of the recipes, think about someone in your community who could use the extra portions. Maybe a single parent, someone who has had a rough week or a family struggling financially would be blessed to receive that meal.

12.) Don't you feel restricted on what you can eat?

I thought about this one for a while. Although socially it may be restricting at times, I do not feel restricted in my own home. I compiled a list of the foods which I enjoyed in my omnivore days and compared it to the foods which I discovered after switching to a plant-based diet. This second list, by the way, continues to grow each week. I think you will be as shocked as I was that the foods I gave up are far fewer than the foods I have discovered. Also, take special note, if there are foods you do not recognize on my Foods Discovered list below, give them a try. Pick one or two new things each week or month to try. Some things you'll love and others you won't and that's okay. Experience them, broaden your palate and enjoy the journey.

Foods Abandoned

bacon	breakfast sausage	butter
cheddar cheese	cheese pizza	cheesy balls/chips
chicken	chicken nuggets/patties	corn dogs
cream cheese	eggnog	eggs
filet mignon	ham	hamburgers
hot dogs	ice cream	marshmallows
mayonnaise	milk	Monterey jack cheese
mozzarella cheese	Munster cheese	parmesan cheese
pepperoni	pepperoni pizza	pot roast
sausage	sour cream	steak, all varieties
sugar	veal	whipped cream
yogurt		

Foods Discovered

açaí	agave nectar	almond butter
amaranth	arrowroot powder	arugula
avocado	beans, all varieties	beet greens
beets	bok choy	buckwheat
cactus pear	cashew butter	celeriac
cherimoya	chia seeds	coconut meat, young
coconut milk	coconut milk beverage	coconut milk eggnog
coconut milk ice cream	coconut milk yogurt	coconut water, young
collard greens	coriander	cumin
curry	dandelion leaves	dulse
durian	eight ball squash	evaporated cane juice
figs	flax seeds	ginger
goji berry	heirloom tomato	jicama
kale, all varieties	kelp	leek
lentils, all varieties	lychee	millet
mulberry	nori seaweed	nutritional yeast
papaya	parsnips	pepitas
polenta	portabella mushroom	quinoa
romanesco broccoli/cauliflower	rutabaga	spaghetti squash
spelt	spirulina	sprouts, all varieties
stevia	Swiss chard	tahini
tofu, all varieties	turmeric	turnips
vegan bacon	vegan butter	vegan cheese
vegan chicken nuggets/patties	vegan cream cheese	vegan mayonnaise
vegan sausages	vegan sour cream	wheatgrass
wild rice		

13.) Are these recipes healthy?

Quite honestly, I don't like hearing the word *healthy* in reference to a recipe. What is the definition of healthy? You can look it up in the dictionary, but when calling a recipe healthy, I believe it is solely a matter of opinion based on your own knowledge and experiences. Do some research, formulate your personal definition and make conscious decisions about how you choose to nourish your body. The only thing I will say about my recipes is that they are plant-based. Are they healthy recipes? You decide.

14.) Which recipes are your favorites?

Here, in no particular order, is my top ten list:

1.) Nonnie's Pasta Sauce (see page 50).
2.) Yellow Elbows (see page 40).
3.) Chocolate Banana Shake (see page 24).
4.) Roasted Veggie Sandwiches with Pesto Aioli (see pages 61-62).
5.) Lazy Pot Pie (see pages 57-58).
6.) Cream of Broccoli Soup (see page 82).
7.) Beverage-Worthy Salsa (see page 101).
8.) Scrappy Meals (see pages 48, 80, 88).
9.) Perfect Pancakes (see page 28).
10.) White Bean Hummus (see page 39).

15.) Are these recipes kid-friendly?

If your kids are used to eating fast food, boxed and frozen pre-made meals, changes may be an adjustment. All of my omnivore recipe testers have had good to great responses from their kids whose ages range from eighteen months to eighteen years old. As far as my kiddo is concerned, whatever I make is usually happily gobbled up. And that leads to the next question...

16.) How does your kid gladly eat anything you make?

Before I got pregnant, I heard from someone that a baby's taste buds start to develop and acquire longings for certain foods while in the womb. Is this true or not? I don't know, but it made sense to me. I thought of all the mothers I've talked to who expressed their frustrations with their children being picky eaters. *IF* babies acquire their tastes while in the womb, then maybe what the mother eats during pregnancy is influential. I committed myself when I became pregnant to eat as many whole foods as I could while minimizing or avoiding processed foods. My naughtiest pleasure was potato chips, so I made sure that during my pregnancy I did not eat them. I produced a child who loves whole foods of all kinds. Did I get lucky? Maybe, but I am willing to do it again during future pregnancies. I'll keep you posted.

17.) Are you an animal activist?

My husband and I went vegan solely for the health benefits. The more I read about nutrition in books like *Diet for a New America* by John Robbins and others, the more I've learned about how meals from the Standard American Diet make it to your plate. My heart now aches for those poor creatures that endure unbearable lives and horrifying deaths. What am I talking about? Do yourself a favor. Watch the short video on www.meat.org. It's time to open our eyes.

18.) Do you cook every single night?

Nope. On a good week I may make dinner five or six times but on a busy or lazy week maybe three or four times, if that. Shh!! Some nights we decide to eat at our favorite restaurants. Sometimes we indulge in our favorite pre-made meals. Although they are convenient and delicious, we prefer not to use them very often. There are many options for vegan-friendly, pre-made meals. Here are a few of our favorites:

Chili, sauce, soups:
Amy's® Organic Medium Chili with Vegetables
Amy's® Organic Lentil Soup (my little one's favorite)
Amy's® Organic Minestrone Soup
Amy's® Thai Coconut Soup
Organicville® Marinara Pasta Sauce served with cooked pasta

Bigger meals:
Amy's® Rice Crust Spinach Pizza
Amy's® Roasted Vegetable Pizza
Amy's® Vegan Margherita Pizza
Beyond Meat™ Chicken-Free Strips- Grilled
Health is Wealth® Chicken Free Nuggets
Health is Wealth® Chicken Free Patties
Rising Moon Organics® Butternut Squash Ravioli

19.) What are some examples of a typical weekly menu?

The possibilities are endless. Here are two examples:

WEEK #1

	Saturday	Sunday	Monday	Tuesday	Wednesday	Thursday	Friday
Break-fast	*Super C Smoothie* (page 25) with toast	*Perfect Pancakes* (page 28)	Fresh juice and *Chocolate Banana Shake* (page 24)	Fresh juice and oatmeal	Fresh juice and cereal	Fresh juice and *Chocolate Banana Shake* (page 24)	Fresh juice and *Rice in Milk* (page 30)
Lunch	*Grilled Cheese* (page 38)	Leftovers from night before	Leftovers from night before	Leftovers from night before	Leftovers from night before	Leftovers from night before	Leftovers from night before
Dinner	*White Bean Hummus* (page 39) with whole grain bread and veggies	*Roasted Veggie Sandwiches with Pesto Aioli* (page 61)	*Simple Beans* (page 68) with *Easy Breezy Guacamole* (page 102) and other fixings i.e. brown rice, diced tomatoes	*Pesto Pita Pizzas* (page 41)	*Quinoa and Bean Chili* (page 78)	*Nonnie's Pasta Sauce* (page 50) with pasta or *Painless Polenta* (page 46)	*Baked Potato Dinner* (page 66) with *Quinoa and Bean Chili* leftovers

	Saturday	Sunday	Monday	Tuesday	Wednesday	Thursday	Friday
Break-fast	*Marry Me Muffins* (page 29)	Cereal	Fresh juice and *Parfait* (page 32)	Fresh juice and *Chocolate Banana Shake* (page 24)	Fresh juice and oatmeal	Fresh juice and cereal	Fresh juice and *Chocolate Banana Shake* (page 24)
Lunch	*BLT* (page 37)	Leftovers from night before	Leftovers from night before	Leftovers from night before	Leftovers from night before	Leftovers from night before	Leftovers from night before
Din-ner	*Yellow Elbows* (page 40) with a simple salad	*Sloppy Joe's Cousin with Syracuse Salt Potatoes* (page 69)	*Spinach Tofu Lasagna* (page 63) with a simple salad	*Lazy Pot Pie* (page 57)	*Bulgur Enchilada Casserole* (page 64)	*Cream of Broccoli Soup* (page 82)	*Savory Quinoa* (page 76)

20.) Have any questions?

Please check out my website at IAmQuamo.com or e-mail me at Jaclyn@IAmQuamo.com and ask away! No question is a silly question.

Breakfast

Date Tried: 1/15/2018   Winner: Yes ✓ No ___

Chocolate Banana Shake

Makes 2 to 4 servings

This is a breakfast staple in our household. When we are feeling lazy, it makes a great dinner, too!

3 cups frozen bananas, diced*
2 cups non-dairy milk
$\frac{1}{8}$ to $\frac{1}{4}$ cup agave nectar
2 heaping Tbsp. cacao or cocoa powder

In a blender, pulse all ingredients together, then puree until smooth.

*The best time to freeze bananas is when they start to form brown spots on the outside. After peeling the banana, break off small chunks and then gently squeeze around the flesh. It should naturally separate into three segments. Put the segments into a quart-sized re-sealable plastic freezer bag and place down flat in the freezer overnight. No need to dirty a knife in the process.

See variation on page 98.

Super C Smoothie
Makes 2 to 4 servings

This light smoothie is jam-packed with vitamin C to take your sniffles away. Enjoy with a side of whole grain toast. If you like things on the sweeter side, replace the water with more apple juice.

½ to 1 cup water
1 cup apple juice
1 cup frozen blueberries
1 cup frozen cherries
1 (3.5 oz.) Sambazon® Immunity Smoothie Pack Açaí Berry + Acerola, frozen

In a blender, combine all ingredients and blend until smooth.

Get Your Greens Smoothie
Makes 2 to 4 servings

I am not much of a salad person. I prefer to drink my greens. Am I a cheater? Maybe, but I'm okay with that. There are so many options for a green smoothie. Here is just one of them.

1 cup or more of water until desired consistency
2 medium bananas
1 cup frozen peaches
1 cup frozen mango
2 to 4 large handfuls of fresh spinach
Agave nectar, to taste

In a blender, combine all ingredients and blend until smooth.

Date Tried: _____   Winner: Yes ___ No ___

Brown Rice-Pumpkin Seed Milk
Makes 1 gallon

This takes some time, approximately seven hours, but you can save some money. Be sure to start soaking the pumpkin seeds a few hours before you start cooking the rice. Use it for cereal or any of your non-dairy milk needs.

1 cup uncooked long-grain brown rice
8 cups water, plus more for diluting
¼ tsp. sea salt
1 cup pumpkin seeds, soaked for 7 hours, then drained and rinsed
2 Tbsp. flaxseed oil
$^1/_3$ cup agave nectar

In a large pot, bring the rice and water to a boil over high heat. Cover, then lower the heat to a simmer. Cook the rice for three hours. The rice mixture will look soupy. Remove from heat and mix in the salt. In batches, fill a blender halfway with some of the rice mixture and halfway with additional water. Blend until smooth. Strain into a very large bowl using a fine mesh strainer, cheese cloth, or a nut bag* and massage to get the milk out. There will be leftover pulp in the straining vessel; discard, rinse out, and then reuse. Repeat until all of the rice mixture is used up. In one of the batches, include the soaked pumpkin seeds and flaxseed oil. Stir the agave nectar into the milk for about one minute. Add additional water if too thick. Using a funnel, carefully pour your milk into mason jars or a closed container of choice. This will last about 5 to 7 days in the refrigerator.

*Do an internet search or look in your local health food store for nut bags. I love these things. It makes recipes like this one so much easier.

Perfect Pancakes
Makes approximately 9 pancakes

This is my favorite pancake recipe. If you are entertaining, have some fresh blueberries or vegan chocolate chips, such as Enjoy Life® Semi-Sweet Chocolate Mini Chips, on hand to add on as toppings.

1 $^2/_3$ cups whole wheat flour
$^1/_3$ cup rolled oats
1½ tsp. baking powder
½ tsp. baking soda
2 Tbsp. evaporated cane juice
½ tsp. sea salt
5 ½ Tbsp. Earth Balance® Natural Buttery Spread, chilled
2⅔ 3 cups non-dairy milk
2 tsp. apple cider vinegar

In a large bowl, combine the flour, rolled oats, baking powder, baking soda, evaporated cane juice and salt. Mix well. Add the butter and cut in with a fork or pastry blender until the mixture has a sand-like consistency. In a separate small bowl, combine the milk and vinegar, lightly stir together. Pour the milk mixture into the flour mixture. Stir together gently until just mixed. Portion the batter using a ladle onto a griddle or non-stick skillet on medium heat. At this time, lightly sprinkle your toppings onto your pancake (see note above). Cook until bubbles appear and the pancake becomes sturdy. Flip it over with a spatula and cook until golden brown. Repeat process until the batter is gone.

Marry Me Muffins
Makes 12 muffins

I constantly tease my co-worker Gene about not getting married to the love of his life. When he tasted this muffin recipe, he was so enthusiastic about it that I replied, "I bet you'd marry these muffins if you could, huh?" We both had a giggle and, hence, the name of the recipe. Using the white bean puree in place of oil makes these muffins practically fat free.

1½ cups whole wheat flour
½ cup evaporated cane juice
1 tsp. sea salt
2 tsp. baking powder
¾ cup non-dairy milk
¼ cup white bean puree (see page 11)
1 cup frozen blueberries

Preheat oven to 400°F (204°C). Line your muffin pan with baking cups. In a large bowl, combine flour, evaporated cane juice, salt and baking powder. Add the milk and the bean puree. Mix well to incorporate all ingredients. Gently fold in the blueberries. Spoon the batter into baking cups and bake for 25 to 30 minutes.

See variation on page 108.

Rice in Milk
Makes 1 serving

I always get weird looks when I eat this, but I don't care. I grew up eating this for breakfast. My sisters and I love it. Plus, it's a perfect way to use leftover rice!

Plain cooked brown rice, cooled
Non-dairy milk
Evaporated cane juice

Prepare this as you would a bowl of cereal. Add as much rice, milk and evaporated cane juice to your bowl as you would like.

Deliciously Dense Donuts
Makes 12 donuts

The whole wheat flour gives these donuts a dense, cake-like texture but no one seems to mind when I hand out samples. Some may want to decrease the amount of nutmeg while increasing the cinnamon.

2 cups whole wheat flour
¼ cup flax seeds, finely ground
¾ cup evaporated cane juice, plus more for topping
2 tsp. baking powder
1 tsp. sea salt
¼ tsp. nutmeg
¼ tsp. cinnamon
1 tsp. extra-virgin olive oil
1 medium banana, mashed
¾ cup non-dairy milk
1 tsp. vanilla extract

Preheat oven to 325°F (163°C). Lightly grease donut pan with extra-virgin olive oil. In a large bowl, combine flour, ground flax seeds, evaporated cane juice, baking powder, salt, nutmeg and cinnamon. Add the oil, banana, milk and vanilla. Mix until well blended. Fill each donut cavity two-thirds full. Lightly sprinkle the tops of donuts with additional evaporated cane juice. Bake 12 to 14 minutes or until tops spring back when lightly touched. Cool and then remove donuts from pan. Wipe pan clean with a damp cloth and then repeat the process with remaining donut batter.

Parfait
Makes 4 servings

A simple change to non-dairy yogurt makes this breakfast possible. If you use large berries like strawberries, make sure to dice them up into bite-size pieces. When choosing granola, stay away from those with honey as vegans prefer not to use it.

2 cups plain non-dairy yogurt
2 cups granola
2 cups fresh or frozen berries, i.e., blueberries, raspberries, etc.

Layer ingredients in four large glass cups as follows: first, ¼ cup of the non-dairy yogurt in each cup, ¼ cup of the granola on top of the yogurt, followed by ¼ cup of the berries. Repeat the process.

Sausage Gravy and Low-Fat Biscuits
Makes 4 servings

Yes, folks, this gravy got the thumbs up sign from several omnivores.

2 Tbsp. extra-virgin olive oil
1 (14 oz.) package Lightlife™ Gimme Lean® Sausage
¼ cup whole wheat flour
2 cups non-dairy milk
Sea salt, to taste
8 low-fat biscuits (see recipe on next page)

In a medium non-stick pan, heat oil over medium heat and squeeze sausage into pan. Break apart with a spatula and sauté until golden brown, about 10 minutes. Stir in flour then gradually add milk, stirring constantly. Add salt and then cook until gravy is thick. Serve immediately over biscuits.

Low-Fat Biscuits
Makes 8 biscuits

Warning: these are NOT the light and fluffy biscuits you grew up on. I repeat: these are NOT the light and fluffy biscuits you grew up on because they are made with whole wheat flour and white bean puree instead of butter. I cut a biscuit in half, add a small dab of vegan butter to each side and smother with the gravy. If you miss the fat, substitute the bean puree for the same amount of vegan butter.

2 cups whole wheat flour
½ tsp. sea salt
4 tsp. baking powder
½ tsp. cream of tarter
2 tsp. evaporated cane juice
½ cup white bean puree (see page 11)
¾ cup non-dairy milk

Preheat oven to 450°F (232°C). In a large bowl, add the flour, salt, baking powder, cream of tartar and evaporated cane juice and then sift together. Mix in the bean puree until well incorporated. Add the milk and stir until dough forms a ball. On a lightly floured surface, press dough together and then form a 4-inch-wide roll. Cut 1-inch thick biscuits and place on a baking sheet lightly greased with extra-virgin olive oil. Bake for 10 minutes or until golden brown.

Breakfast Cookies
Makes about 18 cookies

What a way to start the day- unless you run into the problem of making them the night before and not having any left by morning.

1 cup raw walnuts, chopped
1 ½ cups old-fashioned rolled oats (not instant)
$^1/_3$ cup whole wheat flour
½ cup flax seeds, finely ground
1 tsp. baking soda
½ tsp. sea salt
1 tsp. ground cinnamon
½ cup almond butter

¼ cup white bean puree (see page 11)
¼ cup agave nectar
¼ cup evaporated cane juice
½ medium banana, mashed
1 tsp. vanilla extract
½ cup dried cranberries
½ to 1 cup semi-sweet vegan chocolate chips

Preheat oven to 375°F (191°C). Line two baking sheets with parchment paper. In a food processor, pulse walnuts until they resemble coarse salt. Transfer to a large bowl. Add the oats, flour, ground flax seeds, baking soda, salt and cinnamon, then mix to combine. In a medium bowl, add the almond butter, bean puree, agave nectar, evaporated cane juice, banana and vanilla extract, stir until well combined. To the almond butter mixture, fold in the dried cranberries and chocolate chips. Pour the almond butter mixture into the oat mixture and stir until well combined. Grease a ¼ cup measuring cup lightly with extra-virgin olive oil then scoop and drop the batter onto the prepared baking sheets about 2 inches apart. Bake for 10 to 12 minutes.

Quick and Simple Meals

BLT

Makes 3 sandwiches

I was a vegan for a while before I realized that I could eat these, too. I was in heaven. I thought I had given them up forever. Instead of lettuce, I use fresh spinach.

1 (6 oz.) package Lightlife™ Smoky Tempeh Strips, Fakin' Bacon®
6 slices whole wheat bread
Earth Balance® Natural Buttery Spread (optional)
Earth Balance® Olive Oil MindfulMayo™ Dressing & Sandwich Spread (optional)
Lettuce or spinach leaves
1 tomato, sliced

Cook the Fakin' Bacon® according to the package instructions. Toast the bread and spread with butter or MindfulMayo™. Assemble Fakin Bacon®, lettuce and tomato as desired.

Grilled Cheese
Makes 1 sandwich

I'm not typically a fan of vegan cheeses, but I do gladly use the one mentioned below.

2 to 3 Tbsp. Daiya® cheddar style shreds
2 slices whole wheat bread
Earth Balance® Natural Buttery Spread

Heat a non-stick skillet on medium heat. Meanwhile, sprinkle cheese on one slice of bread. Place the second slice of bread on top of the cheese. Butter the top slice of bread and place in the heated skillet, butter side down. Fry for 3 to 5 minutes or until browned. Meanwhile, butter the top of the sandwich. Flip with a spatula and fry for an additional 3 minutes or until golden brown and the cheese is melted.

Variation: use leftover Spinach Basil Pesto (see page 62) and spread a layer onto a slice of your bread before adding the cheese.

White Bean Hummus
Makes about 4 cups

This doesn't use the traditional garbanzo beans but, to me, great northern white beans make all the difference. Enjoy with crackers, veggies or make a sandwich on whole wheat bread with fresh veggies. Only have garbanzo beans in your pantry? Simply replace the white beans with garbanzo beans.

2 (15 oz.) cans or 3 cups cooked great northern white beans, drained and rinsed
6 garlic cloves, minced
½ cup tahini
6 Tbsp. extra-virgin olive oil
¼ cup lemon juice
1 Tbsp. + ½ tsp. Braggs® Liquid Aminos or soy sauce
1 ½ tsp. sea salt
1½ tsp. cumin
¼ cup or more of cold water until desired consistency

Place all ingredients except cold water into a food processor. Blend until pureed. While the food processor is running, add cold water through the spout. Process for 20 more seconds.

Yellow Elbows
Makes 2 large or 4 small servings

This is my number one standby if I am pressed for time. It is quick, easy and tasty.

8 oz. whole wheat or brown rice elbow macaroni
½ tsp. garlic salt
¼ cup non-dairy milk
¼ cup Earth Balance® Natural Buttery Spread
¼ cup nutritional yeast

In a medium pot of salted water, boil the pasta until al dente. Drain the pasta, return to the pot, then add the remaining ingredients and mix until well incorporated. Serve immediately.

See variation on page 55.

Pita Pizzas

I love pita pizza nights! They are fun for the whole family. Here are just a few of the versions that we enjoy in our home.

Pesto Pita Pizzas
Makes 6 pizzas

Use your leftover Spinach Basil Pesto from the Roasted Veggie Sandwiches (see page 62). We also use any leftover roasted veggies to top this pizza. Topping ideas are endless but here is our basic list:

6 whole wheat pitas
Pesto (see note above)
Roasted vegetables (see note above)
Baby portabella mushrooms, sliced and lightly sautéed in extra-virgin olive oil
Roasted red bell peppers, thinly sliced
Artichoke hearts in brine, drained and quartered
Tomatoes, thinly sliced
Spinach, lightly sautéed in olive oil

Preheat oven to 400°F (204°C). Line two large cookie sheets with aluminum foil. Place three pitas on each cookie sheet. Spread a portion of the pesto onto each pita. Arrange each pita with the desired toppings. Bake for 10 minutes or until crispy.

Black Bean Pita Pizzas

Makes 6 pizzas

Use the leftover beans from the Simple Beans recipe (see page 68).

6 whole wheat pitas
Simple Beans (see note above)
Frozen corn, thawed
Roasted red bell peppers, diced and seeded
Green chiles, diced and seeded
Jalapeño peppers, diced and seeded
Tomatoes, diced
Daiya® cheddar style shreds

Preheat oven to 400°F (204°C). Line two large cookie sheets with aluminum foil.
Place three pitas on each cookie sheet. Mash the beans with a fork and spread a
portion of the bean mash onto each pita. Arrange each pita with the desired toppings.
Bake for 10 minutes or until crispy.

Salsa Pita Pizzas
Makes 6 pizzas

Use leftover salsa, such as Beverage-Worthy Salsa (see page 101), from your last Mexican-style dinner.

6 whole wheat pitas
Salsa (see note above)
Black beans, cooked or canned, drained and rinsed
Frozen corn, thawed
Roasted red bell peppers, diced and seeded
Green chiles, diced and seeded
Jalapeño peppers, diced and seeded
Tomatoes, diced
Daiya® cheddar style shreds

Preheat oven to 400°F (204°C). Line two large cookie sheets with aluminum foil. Place three pitas on each cookie sheet. Spread a portion of the salsa onto each pita. Arrange each pita with the desired toppings. Bake for 10 minutes or until crispy.

Cheese Pita Pizzas

Makes 6 pizzas

Yes, indeed, vegans can have a version of a cheese pizza. My husband can never resist. Be sure that the pizza sauce contains no dairy. Our favorites are the organic pizza sauces from Muir Glen® and Organicville®.

6 whole wheat pitas
Pizza sauce
Daiya® mozzarella style shreds

Preheat oven to 400°F (204°C). Line two large cookie sheets with aluminum foil. Place three pitas on each cookie sheet. Spread a portion of the pizza sauce onto each pita. Top each pita with $^1/_8$ to ¼ cup of cheese. Bake for 10 minutes or until crispy.

Apples, Almonds and Agave Oh My!
Makes 1 serving

Super simple!! This is for those nights when you are solo and have no energy. I've eaten this many times. So, go ahead, be lazy, I won't tell a soul.

$^1/_3$ cup almond butter
Agave nectar, to taste
2 to 3 apples, cored and sliced

In a small bowl, mix the almond butter with the desired amount of agave nectar. Dip the apple slices and enjoy.

Painless Polenta
Makes 4 to 6 servings

Never made polenta before? Have no fear! This is super simple and quick. Serve with Nonnie's Pasta Sauce (see page 50) and sautéed veggies. Spread leftover polenta in a 9 x 13-inch baking dish, cover with plastic wrap and place in the fridge. The next day cut out squares and pan fry in a little vegan butter and serve with leftover chili or legumes.

3 cups non-dairy milk
1 Tbsp. Earth Balance® Natural Buttery Spread
1 tsp. agave nectar
½ tsp. sea salt
1 cup stone-ground yellow cornmeal

In a medium saucepan, combine milk, butter, agave nectar and salt over medium heat until it simmers. Reduce the heat to low, then slowly add the cornmeal while whisking constantly. Continue whisking until the mixture has thickened, about 5 to 10 minutes. Serve immediately.

Hubby's Taco Dinner
Makes 8 to 10 servings

In the words of my favorite boy, "everything tastes better with BBQ sauce!" Serve with your favorite taco fixings, i.e. salsa, guacamole, diced tomatoes, beans, shredded lettuce, brown rice.

2 Tbsp. extra-virgin olive oil or Italian dressing
1 jalapeño pepper, diced (optional)
2 (12 oz.) packages Lightlife™ Smart Ground® Mexican Style
1 to 2 Tbsp. taco seasoning such as Simply Organic® Southwest Taco (optional)
$1/3$ cup BBQ sauce such as Annie's® Naturals Organic Original BBQ Sauce
Dash of cayenne pepper (optional)

In a large skillet, heat oil or dressing over medium heat and add jalapeño pepper. Sauté for 3 to 5 minutes, then add Smart Ground®, break apart and cook for 4 to 6 minutes. Add taco seasoning, BBQ sauce and cayenne and then stir to combine. Cook an additional 3 minutes and then serve immediately.

Date Tried: _____   Winner: Yes ___ No ___

Scrappy Meal #1
Makes 1 serving

Here is a great way to use leftovers: stuff them in a quesadilla! I like going non-traditional and filling it with leftover mashed potatoes, legumes and veggies. Any legumes, grains or veggies will do. To help contain the filling, I use one tortilla folded in half. I like to use sprouted tortillas or something with as few ingredients as possible. Make sure the tortillas don't contain fish oil or honey.

½ tsp. Earth Balance® Natural Buttery Spread
1 whole wheat tortilla
Leftovers of choice
1 to 2 Tbsp. Daiya® cheddar style shreds

In a large non-stick skillet, heat the butter over medium heat. Place the tortilla in the skillet. Fill with leftovers of choice on one half of the tortilla. Sprinkle with cheese. Fold the tortilla over onto filling. Cook for 3 to 5 minutes and then flip. Cook for an additional 3 minutes or until filling is warmed through and cheese is melted. Cut into three sections and serve.

Oodles of Noodles

Nonnie's Pasta Sauce
Makes 4 to 6 servings

No one will ever come close to recreating my Nonnie's sauce, but here is a vegan version that definitely puts a smile on my face. The first time I made this was a very emotional experience for me because it felt as if she was right there in the kitchen guiding me along. I miss you, Nonnie!

4 Field Roast® Italian Sausages, casings removed and finely diced
$1/3$ cup extra-virgin olive oil
1 small onion, diced
3 (14.5 oz.) cans crushed tomatoes*
1 (6 oz.) can tomato paste
¼ tsp. garlic powder
1 tsp. sea salt
4 to 6 garlic cloves, peeled and whole
$1/8$ tsp. dried parsley
$1/8$ tsp. dried oregano
$1/8$ tsp. Italian seasoning

In a medium pot, brown the sausages in the oil on medium heat. Add the onion and sauté until lightly browned. Add the remaining ingredients. Cover and simmer on low heat for an hour, stirring occasionally. Serve with your favorite cooked pasta.

*If you only have canned diced tomatoes, simply pour them into your blender, then pulse two or three times.

Goulash
Makes 8 servings

The Field Roast® Chipotle Sausages make this meatless goulash a bit spicy. Serve with Sweet Cornbread (see page 92).

2 Tbsp. extra-virgin olive oil

2 large onions, diced

3 garlic cloves, minced

2 red bell peppers, seeded and chopped

3 cups low sodium tomato juice

2 (15 oz.) cans tomato sauce

2 (14.5 oz.) cans diced tomatoes

2 cups frozen corn

4 Field Roast® Chipotle Sausages, casings removed and finely diced

1 Tbsp. vegan Worcestershire sauce

2 Tbsp. Bragg's® Liquid Aminos or soy sauce

2 Tbsp. Italian seasoning

3 bay leaves

1 Tbsp. sea salt

2 ½ cups uncooked whole wheat or brown rice elbow macaroni

In a large pot, heat the oil over medium heat. Sauté the onions and garlic until the onions are translucent. Add the peppers and sauté an additional 3 to 5 minutes. Add the tomato juice, tomato sauce, diced tomatoes, corn, sausages, Worcestershire sauce, liquid aminos or soy sauce, Italian seasoning, bay leaves and salt. Bring to a boil, then reduce heat to low, cover, and simmer for 20 minutes, stirring occasionally. Meanwhile, cook the elbow macaroni in a separate pot according to package instructions. Drain and then add to the sauce mixture. Stir until well combined. Remove from heat, discard the bay leaves and serve.

Spicy Tomato Peanut Pasta
Makes 4 to 6 servings

I have always loved eating peanut butter on bread with my pasta. Now I can get the best of both worlds in one dish.

1 lb. whole wheat penne
2 (15 oz.) cans tomato sauce
2 cups kale, finely chopped
¼ cup non-hydrogenated peanut butter
2 tsp. Asian chili-garlic sauce, or more to taste
½ cup peanuts, dry roasted and salted

In a large pot of salted water, boil the pasta according to the package instructions. Drain. Meanwhile, in a large saucepan over medium heat, pour in the tomato sauce and bring to a simmer, then add kale, cook for 2 to 3 minutes until kale is bright green. Add the peanut butter and Asian chili-garlic sauce and stir until well incorporated. Simmer for 2 minutes. Add the pasta and peanuts to the sauce mixture and gently mix together.

College Noodles
Makes 4 servings

Every time I eat this it reminds me of sitting at the table with my sisters and cousins eating ramen noodles while egging each other on to add even more hot sauce. With sweaty brows and runny noses, great memories were had by all. Enjoy with a peanut butter and jelly sandwich. Continue the tradition: add your favorite hot sauce for a spicy kick.

6 cups water
1 (8 oz.) package baby portabella mushrooms, thinly sliced
2 stalks celery, thinly sliced
2 medium carrots, thinly sliced
1 (8 oz.) package Annie Chun's® Maifun Brown Rice Noodles or any rice noodle
¼ cup Bragg's® Liquid Aminos or soy sauce
1 Tbsp. dried parsley
2 tsp. onion powder
2 Tbsp. dehydrated minced onion
½ tsp. garlic powder
Hot sauce, to taste (optional)

Bring the water to a boil in a medium-size pot. Add the mushrooms, celery and carrots and boil for 6 minutes. Add the noodles and boil for an additional 3 to 4 minutes or until noodles are soft. Add the remaining ingredients to the pot and stir until well incorporated. Remove from heat and set aside for 5 minutes before serving.

Enchilada Pasta

Makes 4 servings

Because it uses fresh ingredients, I use Frontera® Red Chile Enchilada Sauce with roasted tomato and garlic. If you can't find this and don't want to buy it on-line, read the labels! Many other enchilada sauces have meat flavoring, a vegan no-no; others also have monosodium glutamate (MSG) and corn syrup byproducts which I choose not to use in my home.

1 lb. whole wheat shell macaroni
2 Tbsp. extra-virgin olive oil
2 large red bell peppers, seeded and diced
2 medium onions, diced
1 jalapeño pepper, seeded and diced
2 (8 oz.) packages Frontera® Red Chile Enchilada Sauce
1 (16 oz.) can vegetarian refried beans

1 (15 oz.) can or 1 ½ cups cooked black beans, drained and rinsed
3 Tbsp. Simply Organic® Southwest Taco seasoning
1 tsp. sea salt
½ cup Daiya® cheddar style shreds
2 cups Kettle Brand Tias!™ Salsa Picante tortilla chips, crushed

Cook shell macaroni according to package instructions; drain and set aside. Meanwhile, in a large skillet, heat oil over medium heat and add bell peppers, onions and jalapeño. Sauté for about 5 minutes or until onions are translucent. Stir in enchilada sauce and refried beans until well combined. Then add black beans, taco seasoning, salt and cheese. Reduce the heat to low and simmer uncovered for 5 minutes. Gently toss pasta with sauce mixture. Garnish with crushed tortilla chips.

Beef Up Your Yellow Elbows
Makes 6 servings

Ok, you're not going crazy. You are seeing double! I simply doubled the ingredients from Yellow Elbows found on page 40. Below you'll find some ideas to add a little more bulk to this dish.

1 lb. whole wheat or brown rice elbow macaroni
1 tsp. garlic salt
½ cup non-dairy milk
½ cup Earth Balance® Natural Buttery Spread
½ cup nutritional yeast

In a large pot of salted water, boil the pasta until al dente. Drain the pasta, return to the pot, then add the remaining ingredients and mix until well incorporated. Gently mix with any beefy add-ins (see below). Serve immediately.

Beefy add-ins:

Your favorite Field Roast® Sausages, casings removed then diced and sautéed
Fresh tomatoes, diced
1 (15 oz.) can of your favorite beans, drained and rinsed
Your favorite green vegetable, diced and sautéed (i.e. asparagus, broccoli)
Mushrooms, diced and sautéed

Oven Lovin'

Lazy Pot Pie
Makes two 9 inch pot pies

I love being in the kitchen but not to make pie crusts. Instead, I enjoy the convenience of pre-made. Don't worry about the pie shells; they will magically thaw and form a nice crust over the veggie filling. If you must make your own crust or you can't find the pre-made version, use the recipe on the next page.

1 large onion, diced

2 Tbsp. extra-virgin olive oil

4 stalks celery, diced

2 carrots, diced

2 medium potatoes, finely diced

$^2/_3$ cup frozen peas

$^1/_2$ cup red lentils, picked over and rinsed

2 cups vegan vegetable broth

1 tsp. sea salt

½ tsp. dried sage

½ tsp. dried thyme

¼ cup whole wheat flour

1 cup non-dairy milk

2 Wholly Wholesome™ Organic Whole Wheat 9" Pie Shells, frozen

Preheat oven to 400°F (204°C). In a large pan on medium heat, sauté the onion in oil until translucent. Add the celery and carrots and sauté for an additional 3 to 5 minutes. Add the potatoes, peas, lentils, broth, salt, sage and thyme. Bring to a boil, then reduce heat, cover and simmer for 8 minutes. Stir in flour and milk and simmer until sauce begins to thicken. Transfer vegetable mixture to two pie pans. Remove Wholly Wholesome™ Organic Whole Wheat Pie Shells from plastic and pie tin and then gently place pie shells bottom side down on top of cooked vegetables. Once the pie shell is soft enough, make a small 'X' in the center of the dough. Bake for 20 to 25 minutes.

Whole Wheat Pie Crust
Makes two 9 inch pie crusts

The more I make this recipe, the less I dislike making pie crusts! I've found a winner.

2 cups whole wheat flour
1 tsp. sea salt
¾ cup Earth Balance® Natural Buttery Spread
½ cup ice water, or more as needed

In a medium bowl, combine flour and salt. Cut in butter with a fork or pastry blender until it has a sand-like consistency. Gradually add water and mix until the flour mixture forms a ball and cleans the sides of the bowl. Transfer dough to a lightly floured surface and divide in half. With a rolling pin, roll out the first half of the dough to a circle to fit over a 9-inch pie pan. Set aside. Repeat the rolling process to form the second crust.

Date Tried: _____   Winner: Yes ___ No ✓ *men*

Gram's Rice Casserole
Makes 6 to 8 servings

When we first got married and were still omnivores, we spent Thanksgiving dinner with my in-laws. I quickly realized how much my husband loved his Gram's rice casserole. When we went vegan, I recreated the recipe so that his holiday tradition could continue.

1 ½ cups long-grain brown rice
3 cups vegan vegetable broth
1 Tbsp. extra-virgin olive oil
1 (8 oz.) package baby portabella mushrooms, sliced
2 Tbsp. white cooking wine

1 (14.1 oz.) can Amy's® Organic Split Pea Soup
1 cup non-dairy milk
1 ½ cups broccoli florets, chopped
1 ¼ tsp. sea salt
1 ½ cups crispy fried onions

Preheat oven to 350°F (177°C). In a large pot, bring the brown rice and broth to a boil, then reduce heat, cover and simmer for 30 to 40 minutes or until rice is done. Meanwhile, in a medium pan, heat the oil on medium heat. Add the mushrooms and sauté until the mushrooms have browned. Deglaze with the white cooking wine until wine has evaporated. Add mushrooms to the large pot of cooked rice. In the same medium pan on medium heat, warm up the soup and milk to slightly boiling and then add broccoli, salt, and ³/₄ cup of crispy fried onions. Cook for 3 to 5 minutes until broccoli is bright green. Add the soup mixture to the large pot of cooked rice. Mix until well incorporated. Pour into a 2-quart casserole dish. Top with the remaining crispy fried onions. Bake uncovered for 30 minutes. Allow to cool for 10 minutes and then serve.

Baked Ziti
Makes 4 to 6 servings

My anti-vegan brother-in-law tried this recipe and fell in love with it. Enough said.

1 Tbsp. extra-virgin olive oil
2 garlic cloves, minced
2 (8 oz.) packages baby portabella or button mushrooms, sliced
Sea salt, to taste
1 lb. whole wheat ziti or penne, cooked
1 recipe Nonnie's Pasta Sauce (see page 50)
$^1/_3$ to $^2/_3$ cup Daiya® mozzarella style shreds (optional)

Preheat oven to 350°F (177°C). Heat oil in a large sauté pan and then add garlic, sauté for one minute. Add mushrooms and salt and sauté until mushrooms are soft. In a large bowl, combine the pasta, pasta sauce, and mushroom mixture until well incorporated. Place pasta mixture in a 2-quart casserole dish. Sprinkle with cheese. Bake for 15 to 20 minutes. To melt the cheese, broil on high for 2 to 3 minutes.

Roasted Veggie Sandwiches with Pesto Aioli
Makes 6 servings

We eat this on a weekly basis. Based on preference and season, the veggies are interchangeable. Occasionally we use ciabatta bread.

3 medium sweet potatoes, sliced length-wise, ¼-inch thick
2 red bell peppers, seeded and sliced length-wise, 1-inch thick
4 carrots, cut into 4-inch sticks
4 small zucchini, sliced length-wise, ½-inch thick
Extra-virgin olive oil
Sea salt, to taste
Favorite fresh or dried herbs, i.e., basil, oregano, thyme
1 large heirloom tomato, sliced
Whole grain bread

Preheat oven to 400°F (204°C). Line two large cookie sheets with aluminum foil. In a large bowl, toss sweet potatoes, red peppers, carrots, and zucchini with a small amount of oil, salt and herbs individually. Line the vegetables in a single layer onto cookie sheet.   Bake for 30 minutes or until you can poke through the sweet potatoes with a fork. Serve vegetables and tomato slices on toasted whole grain bread or a bun spread with Pesto Aioli (see recipe on the next page).

Spinach Basil Pesto
Makes 24 servings

To be truthful, I have a favorite vegan pesto, Basiltops® Dairy Free Pesto Perfectto, which I purchase at the store. Whenever I am out of town, I use this pesto recipe as a base for the aioli.

1 ½ cups baby spinach leaves	¾ tsp. sea salt
¾ cup fresh basil leaves	1 Tbsp. lemon juice
½ cup raw walnuts	½ tsp. lemon zest
3 garlic cloves, minced	½ cup extra-virgin olive oil

Blend the spinach, basil, walnuts, garlic, salt, lemon juice, lemon zest and a small amount of the oil in a food processor until nearly smooth. Scrape the sides of the processor with a spatula if necessary. Add the remaining oil a little at a time into the mixture while processing until smooth.

Any extra Spinach Basil Pesto can be frozen in ice cube trays covered with plastic wrap. Once frozen, pop the cubes into a freezer bag and keep in the freezer until you need some more pesto.

Pesto Aioli

I like the ratio of 2:1, pesto to vegan mayonnaise. Mix together ½ cup of pesto to ¼ cup vegan mayonnaise in a small bowl. For vegan mayonnaise, we like to use Earth Balance® Olive Oil MindfulMayo™ Dressing & Sandwich Spread.

Spinach Tofu Lasagna
Makes 4 to 6 servings

Tofu and I have a strained relationship. I've never been that much of a fan, but I do make a few exceptions; this recipe is one of them.

1 (16 oz.) package silken tofu, drained and pressed*
1 (10 oz.) package frozen chopped spinach, thawed and squeezed of extra moisture
1 Tbsp. + ¾ tsp. dehydrated minced onion
¾ tsp. sea salt
1½ tsp. garlic powder
1½ tsp. dried oregano
1½ tsp. dried basil
1 (10 oz.) package Follow your Heart® Vegan Gourmet Mozzarella Cheese Alternative, shredded
1 (24 oz.) jar Organicville® Marinara Pasta Sauce
1 (12 oz.) package whole wheat lasagna noodles

Preheat oven to 350°F (177°C). In a large mixing bowl, combine tofu, spinach, onion, salt, garlic powder, oregano, basil and all but two handfuls of the cheese--save the two handfuls for later use. In a 9 x 13-inch baking dish, start with a small layer of spaghetti sauce, then a single layer of noodles, and tofu mixture. Repeat layers until all tofu mixture is gone. Top with remaining spaghetti sauce and then the reserved cheese. Bake for 45 minutes.

*To press tofu, wrap tofu in paper towels on a clean surface such as a cutting board. Place a heavy object on top, possibly a sauté pan filled with heavy objects such as cans, bundles of bananas, etc. Set aside for 5 to 10 minutes to absorb any excess moisture.

Date Tried: _____   Winner: Yes ___ No ___

Bulgur Enchilada Casserole
Makes 4 to 6 servings

This is a yummy way to use bulgur!

1 large onion, diced
¼ cup Italian salad dressing
2 cups bulgur, cooked*
1 cup Beverage-Worthy Salsa (see page 101) or store-bought salsa
1 cup canned green chiles, diced
1 (19 oz.) can or 2 cups cooked black beans, drained and rinsed
2 Tbsp. Simply Organic® Southwest Taco seasoning

¼ tsp. cumin
Sea salt, to taste
8 corn tortillas
1 (6 oz.) container plain non-dairy yogurt
1 cup Daiya® cheddar style shreds
1 cup lettuce, shredded
1 medium tomato, chopped
¼ cup fresh cilantro, minced

Preheat oven to 400°F (204°C). In a large skillet, over medium heat, sauté onion in a little of the Italian dressing for 5 minutes or until translucent. Stir in bulgur, salsa, green chiles, beans, remaining Italian dressing, taco seasoning, cumin and salt. Grease a 9 x 13-inch baking dish with extra-virgin olive oil then layer 4 tortillas on the bottom of the dish. Layer with half of each: bulgur mixture, plain yogurt and cheese. Repeat layers. Cover with aluminum foil and bake for 25 minutes. Uncover and bake an additional 5 to 10 minutes or until heated through. Let stand for 5 minutes, and then top with lettuce, tomato and cilantro.

*To cook bulgur, place two cups of water and one cup of uncooked bulgur into a pot. Bring to a boil, then cover and reduce heat to a simmer for 15 minutes or until tender. Drain excess water.

Tamale Pie
Makes 4 to 6 servings

No need to steam any tamales here!

1 Tbsp. extra-virgin olive oil
1 medium onion, diced
1 red bell pepper, seeded and diced
2 garlic cloves, minced
1 (15 oz.) can unsweetened tomato sauce
1 (15 oz.) can pinto beans, drained and rinsed
1 cup frozen corn, thawed

1 tsp. chili powder
1 tsp. cumin
½ tsp. sea salt
Cayenne pepper, to taste
3 cups water
1 cup yellow stone-ground cornmeal
1 Tbsp. lemon juice
1 tsp. mustard
½ tsp. sea salt

Preheat oven to 350°F (177°C). In a large skillet, heat oil on medium-high heat. Add onion, red pepper and garlic and sauté for 5 minutes or until onions are translucent. Add the tomato sauce, beans, corn, chili powder, cumin, salt, and cayenne and cook another 3 minutes. Pour into a 9 x13-inch baking dish. In a small saucepan, boil the water. Add the cornmeal, lemon juice, mustard and salt and stir until mixed. Return to a boil; reduce heat to low and simmer, stirring constantly, until thickened, about 3 to 5 minutes. Pour the cooked cornmeal over the bean mixture. Bake for 30 minutes. Cool for 10 minutes and then serve.

Baked Potato Dinner
Makes 4 servings

Make any leftovers, i.e., Jaclyn's Jambalaya (see page 73), Sloppy Joe's Cousin (see page 69), a perfect topping for your spuds.

4 medium baking potatoes, washed
Extra-virgin olive oil
Sea salt

Preheat oven to 300°F (149°C). Poke the potatoes with a fork or a knife. Rub each potato with about one teaspoon of oil, then with about ½ teaspoon of salt. Place potatoes directly in the oven and bake for 90 minutes or until slightly soft when squeezed. Slice the potatoes down the center and top with vegan butter, your favorite vegetables or leftovers.

The Magical World of Legumes

Simple Beans
Makes 4 servings

Pop your rice in a rice cooker and you have a fast, low-maintenance dinner coming right up! If you find the beans too dry, add a little water or vegan vegetable broth.

2 (15 oz.) cans or 3 cups cooked black beans, drained and rinsed
½ tsp. sea salt
½ tsp. chili powder
1 tsp. cumin
½ cup canned green chiles, diced
1 medium tomato, diced
¼ cup fresh cilantro, minced

In a medium pot, add all the ingredients, except the tomato and cilantro, and simmer on medium-low for 5 to 10 minutes. Serve with cooked brown rice. Garnish with fresh diced tomatoes and cilantro. Put on tortillas.

Sloppy Joe's Cousin with Syracuse Salt Potatoes
Makes 6 servings

I grew up eating Sloppy Joes and salt potatoes. A few simple changes have made these dishes workable in a vegan kitchen.

3 cups water
1 cup green lentils, picked over and rinsed
Sea salt, to taste
1 jalapeño pepper, finely diced (optional)
3 Tbsp. extra-virgin olive oil
1 medium onion, diced
1 red bell pepper, seeded and diced

2 garlic cloves, minced
1 (14.5 oz.) can diced tomatoes
½ (6 oz.) can tomato paste
½ cup ketchup
1 tsp. mustard powder
1 to 2 tsp. chili powder
3 Tbsp. molasses
1 dash vegan Worcestershire sauce
6 whole wheat hamburger buns

In a medium saucepan, combine water, lentils, salt and jalapeño. Bring to a boil over high heat and then reduce to medium-low. Cover and simmer until tender, about 30 minutes. Set aside. Meanwhile, in a large skillet, over medium heat, heat oil. Add onion, red pepper and garlic and sauté until onions are translucent, about 5 minutes. Stir in lentils with their cooking liquid, tomatoes, tomato paste, ketchup, mustard powder, chili powder, molasses, and Worcestershire sauce. Simmer for 5 to 10 minutes until thickened, stirring occasionally. Serve on buns. See Syracuse Salt Potatoes recipe on the next page.

Syracuse Salt Potatoes
Makes 4 to 6 servings

As they have mine, these creamy-centered potatoes will win your heart!

2 lbs. small red new potatoes
6 cups water
¾ cup sea salt
4 Tbsp. Earth Balance® Natural Buttery Spread, melted

In a large pot, combine potatoes, water and salt, stirring until salt is dissolved. Bring to a boil, then reduce heat to a simmer and cook until potatoes are tender but firm, about 15 minutes. Drain and set aside until a thin salt crust forms. Toss in melted butter and serve immediately.

Sweet Dill Carrots

Makes 4 servings

Another side dish. Sweet and salty.

3 cups carrots, sliced
¼ cup Earth Balance® Natural Buttery Spread
¼ cup agave nectar
2 tsp. dried dill
1 tsp. sea salt

In a medium skillet, add carrots with just enough water to cover. Bring to a boil and simmer until carrots are tender. Drain any excess water and then add butter, agave nectar, dill and salt. Toss to coat.

Saucy Chicks
Makes 4 to 6 servings

This Romesco-style dish can be served over your favorite cooked grain.

½ cup raw almonds

1 (28 oz.) can diced tomatoes

3 roasted red bell peppers, store-bought

2 Tbsp. extra-virgin olive oil

1 small onion, finely diced

2 garlic cloves, minced

¼ to ½ tsp. crushed red pepper

¼ cup white cooking wine

2 tsp. red wine vinegar

2 tsp. agave nectar

1 tsp. dried thyme

½ tsp. paprika

½ tsp. sea salt, or to taste

2 (15 oz.) cans or 3 cups cooked chickpeas, drained and rinsed

In a food processor, grind the almonds into a fine sand-like consistency. Pour into a small bowl and set aside. In a blender, puree diced tomatoes and roasted red bell peppers. Set aside. In a large saucepan, heat oil on medium heat and sauté onion, garlic and crushed red peppers until the onions are translucent, about 5 minutes. Pour in the white wine and stir for one minute. Add the tomato puree, vinegar, agave nectar, thyme, paprika and salt. Turn the heat up to medium-high until almost boiling. Lower the heat to a simmer for 10 minutes, stirring occasionally. Add the ground almonds and stir to combine. Then add the chickpeas and simmer, uncovered, until the sauce thickens, about 15 to 20 minutes.

Jaclyn's Jambalaya
Makes 6 to 8 servings

No shrimp, andouille sausage or chicken here, just plant-based goodness in your bowl!

2 Tbsp. extra-virgin olive oil
1 large onion, diced
1 large red bell pepper, seeded and chopped
4 stalks celery, diced
4 Field Roast® Chipotle Sausages, casings removed and finely diced
1 (25 oz.) can kidney beans, drained and rinsed
1 (28 oz.) can diced tomatoes
¼ cup canned green chiles, diced
3 cups vegan vegetable broth, or more as needed
2 tsp. dried oregano
2 tsp. dried parsley
2 tsp. Cajun seasoning
½ tsp. cayenne pepper (optional)
½ tsp. dried thyme
1 cup long-grain white or brown rice

In a large stock pot, heat oil over medium heat and add onion, pepper and celery. Sauté until onions are translucent, about 5 minutes. Add sausages and sauté until browned, about 5 minutes. Add the remaining ingredients and turn the heat to medium-high. Bring to a boil and then reduce to medium-low. Cover and cook for 15 to 30 minutes or until rice is done, adding additional broth as needed.

Going with the Grain

Cuban Rice
Makes 4 to 6 servings

Spicy and simple.

1 Tbsp. extra-virgin olive oil
1 small onion, diced
4 garlic cloves, minced
2 bell peppers, orange, red or yellow, seeded and chopped
2 jalapeño peppers, seeded and diced
1 ½ cups brown jasmine rice
4 cups vegan vegetable broth
½ tsp. dried oregano
1 tsp. sea salt
$^1/_8$ tsp. cayenne pepper
1 (15 oz.) can or 1 ½ cups cooked black or pinto beans, drained and rinsed
2 Tbsp. lime juice

In a large saucepan, sauté onion, garlic, bell peppers and jalapeños in oil over medium-high heat until onions are translucent, about 5 minutes. Add the rice, broth, oregano, salt, cayenne and beans. Bring to a boil, then reduce heat to low, cover and simmer for 20 to 25 minutes or until rice is cooked. Remove from heat and stir in lime juice.

Savory Quinoa
Makes 4 servings

Based on preference and season, the veggies are interchangeable.

1 Tbsp. extra-virgin olive oil
1 small onion, diced
2 garlic cloves, minced
2 stalks celery, finely diced
8 mushrooms, sliced
2 carrots, finely diced
2 small zucchinis, finely chopped
1 cup quinoa, rinsed
2 cups vegan vegetable broth
1 tsp. dried thyme
½ tsp. sea salt

In a large saucepan, sauté the onion, garlic, celery, mushrooms, carrots and zucchinis in oil over medium heat until onions are translucent, about 5 to 8 minutes. Add the quinoa, broth, thyme and salt and stir to combine. Bring to a boil and then reduce heat to medium-low. Cover and simmer for 15 to 20 minutes until quinoa and vegetables are cooked through.

Lemon Paprika Rice
Makes 4 to 6 servings

When I was growing up, one of my favorite dinners to make for my family was a lemon paprika chicken that they still talk about to this day. I tried to capture that flavor profile in this dish. Save a chicken: ride the grain train!

2 Tbsp. extra-virgin olive oil
1 medium onion, diced
2 garlic cloves, minced
4 cups vegan vegetable broth, or more as needed
2 cups long-grain brown rice
1 large lemon, zested and juiced
1 (25 oz.) can kidney beans, rinsed and drained
1 Tbsp. paprika, or more to taste
1 bunch kale, about 3 to 4 cups, finely chopped
Sea salt, to taste

In a large saucepan, sauté the onion and garlic in oil over medium-high heat until the onions are translucent, about 5 minutes. Add the broth, rice, lemon zest, lemon juice, beans and paprika. Bring to a boil, then reduce heat to medium-low, cover, and simmer for 30 to 40 minutes, or until rice is cooked, adding more broth as needed. Add the kale and mix until well combined. Remove from heat and set aside for 5 to 10 minutes until kale is wilted. Season, as needed, with salt.

Quinoa and Bean Chili
Makes 6 to 8 servings

If you are sensitive to spice, feel free to omit the chipotle peppers as they pack quite a punch to the palate.

1 cup quinoa, rinsed
2 cups water
1 Tbsp. extra-virgin olive oil
1 medium onion, diced
4 garlic cloves, minced
1 tsp. chili powder
1 Tbsp. cumin
1 (28 oz.) can crushed tomatoes
2 (15 oz.) cans or 3 cups cooked black
or pinto beans, drained and rinsed

2 bell peppers, orange, red or yellow,
seeded and chopped
1 zucchini, chopped
1 jalapeño pepper, diced
1 Tbsp. chipotle peppers in adobo
sauce, minced (optional)
1 tsp. dried oregano
1 Tbsp. dried cilantro
1 tsp. sea salt, or to taste
1 cup frozen corn

In a medium saucepan, bring the quinoa and water to a boil over high heat. Reduce heat to medium-low, cover and simmer for 15 to 20 minutes or until quinoa is tender. Set aside. Meanwhile, in a large pot, sauté onion and garlic in oil over medium heat until the onions are translucent, about 5 minutes. Add the chili powder and cumin. Stir and cook for one minute. Add the tomatoes, beans, bell peppers, zucchini, jalapeño, chipotle pepper, oregano, cilantro and salt. Mix well and bring to a boil, then reduce heat to medium-low. Cover and simmer for 20 minutes. Add the quinoa and corn and simmer for an additional 5 minutes.

Spanish-Style Rice
Makes 4 servings

Adding a can of your favorite beans can turn this side dish into a one-pot meal.

1 Tbsp. extra-virgin olive oil
1 cup long-grain brown rice
1 medium onion, diced
3 garlic cloves, minced
1 red bell pepper, seeded and chopped
2 cups vegan vegetable broth, or more as needed
1 (14.5 oz.) can diced tomatoes
½ cup canned green chiles, diced
1 (15 oz.) can of favorite beans, drained and rinsed
1 tsp. chili powder
½ tsp. cumin
1 tsp. sea salt

In a medium saucepan, sauté rice, onion, garlic, and bell pepper in oil over medium heat until rice is browned and onions are translucent, stirring often, about five minutes. Stir in broth, tomatoes, green chiles, beans, chili powder, cumin and salt. Cover and simmer at medium-low for 30 to 40 minutes or until rice is cooked, adding more broth as needed.

.

Scrappy Meal #2
Makes 4 servings

I love scrappy meals! Here's another way to clean out the leftover produce and cooked grains in your fridge. Use your imagination and have fun!

1 Tbsp. extra-virgin olive oil
2 cups vegetables, diced, i.e., potato, celery, carrots
2 cups vegan vegetable broth
1 tsp. seasoning of choice, i.e., basil, curry, oregano
1 (14.5 oz.) can diced tomatoes (optional)
2 cups cooked grain, i.e., rice, quinoa, barley

In a large skillet, sauté vegetables in oil over medium-high heat for 5 minutes, stirring often. Add broth, seasoning and tomatoes. Bring to a boil, then reduce heat to medium-low, cover and simmer for 10 minutes or until all vegetables are cooked through. Add grain and cook, uncovered, for an additional 5 minutes.

For Soup Lovers

Cream of Broccoli Soup
Makes 4 to 6 servings

This is a true winner! We started a Christmas dinner tradition of serving this in bread bowls. Double the recipe and have some family or friends over! Many are shocked that it contains no dairy and prefer it over the dairy-loaded version.   Find out for yourself.

1 ½ cups raw cashews
5 cups vegan vegetable broth
2 medium potatoes, finely diced
1 medium onion, diced
5 cups broccoli, chopped
1 tsp. dried basil
1 tsp. sea salt

Place cashews and 1 ½ cups of vegetable broth into a blender. Blend until smooth, about one minute and set aside. In a large pot, add the remaining broth, potatoes, and onion. Bring to a boil and then reduce heat to a simmer. Cover and cook for 5 minutes. Add the broccoli, basil and salt and then return to a simmer. Cover and cook for another 10 minutes or until the potatoes are tender. Stir in the cashew mixture and cook for 2 additional minutes. Remove from heat then transfer half of the soup to a blender and puree until smooth. Return puree back to the pot and mix well. Serve immediately.

Simply Succotash
Makes 6 to 8 servings

I had never liked lima beans, but when you change to eating a plant-based diet, you may give those foods you previously disliked a second chance. In this case, I became a fan!

1 Tbsp. extra-virgin olive oil
2 medium onions, diced
4 garlic cloves, minced
4 stalks celery, diced
2 large carrots, diced
1 (28 oz.) can diced tomatoes
2 cups vegan vegetable broth
4 cups frozen lima beans, thawed
4 cups frozen corn, thawed
¼ cup canned green chiles, diced (optional)
1 tsp. sea salt
2 Tbsp. dried parsley
2 tsp. paprika, dissolved in 2 Tbsp. water

In a large pot, sauté onions and garlic in oil over medium-high heat until onions are translucent, about 5 minutes. Add celery and carrots and sauté another 5 minutes. Add the remaining ingredients and bring to a boil. Then reduce heat to medium-low, cover, and simmer for 20 minutes to blend the flavors.

Italian Wedding Soup

Makes 6 servings

Omitting the meatballs makes this soup easy to serve for a vegan dinner. My recipe tester's reaction was the following: "The soup is awesome. It feels like my tongue is having Christmas morning. Yeah, it's that good."

12 cups vegan vegetable broth
4 Field Roast® Smoked Apple Sage Sausages, casings removed and finely diced
4 cups escarole, thinly sliced
1½ cups whole wheat orzo pasta
1 (15 oz.) can or 1 ½ cups cooked great northern beans, drained and rinsed
2 medium carrots, finely diced
2 stalks celery, finely diced

In a large pot, bring the broth to a boil. Add the remaining ingredients, return to a boil and then reduce heat to medium-low. Cook, uncovered, for 10 minutes or until pasta is al dente, stirring frequently.

We Three Lentils Stew
Makes 10 to 12 servings

If you can't find all three of these lentils, use whichever you can find and substitute the others in equal proportions. This makes a lot, so I love to freeze leftovers for another night. If you can get your hands on smoked salt, it adds another layer of flavor.

1 Tbsp. extra-virgin olive oil
1 large onion, diced
2 medium carrots, diced
2 stalks celery, diced
10 to 12 cups vegan vegetable broth
1 (14.5 oz.) can diced tomatoes
1 cup red lentils, picked over and rinsed
¾ cup green lentils, picked over and rinsed
¾ cup French green lentils, picked over and rinsed
3 cups butternut squash, peeled, seeded and cubed
Smoked salt, to taste (optional)

In a very large pot, sauté onion, carrots and celery in oil over medium-high heat until onions are translucent, about 5 to 8 minutes. Add broth, tomatoes, lentils, squash and smoked salt and bring to a boil. Reduce heat to medium-low, cover, and cook until lentils are soft, about 30 minutes. Stir often to prevent sticking.

Peruvian Purple Soup

Makes 6 servings

Yes, folks, thanks to the purple cabbage, this broth is purple. If you prefer green cabbage, then you'll have to call it Peruvian Green Soup.

1 Tbsp. extra-virgin olive oil
1 medium onion, diced
4 garlic cloves, minced
1 jalapeño pepper, diced
1 large carrot, thinly sliced
8 cups vegan vegetable broth
3 Tbsp. Bragg's® Liquid Aminos or soy sauce
1 cup quinoa, rinsed
2 medium potatoes, cubed
1 ½ cups purple cabbage, sliced
1 (14.5 oz.) can diced tomatoes
2 Tbsp. dried cilantro
2 Tbsp. dried parsley
1 tsp. sea salt

In a large saucepan, sauté onion, garlic, jalapeño and carrot in oil over medium-high heat until onions are translucent, about 5 to 8 minutes. Add the remaining ingredients and bring to a boil. Reduce heat to medium-low, cover and cook for 20 minutes or until the quinoa and vegetables are cooked.

Salsa Soup
Makes 4 to 6 servings

Super quick, super easy and uses leftover rice from your fridge. Win, win, win!

6 cups vegan vegetable broth
2 cups Beverage-Worthy Salsa (see page 101) or 1 (16 oz.) jar of store-bought salsa
1 (15 oz.) can or 1½ cups cooked black beans, drained and rinsed
¼ cup canned green chiles, diced
1 cup frozen corn
1 to 2 tsp. chili powder
1 to 2 cups rice, cooked

Place all ingredients except the rice in a medium saucepan and bring to a boil.
Reduce heat to medium-low and cook uncovered for 10 minutes. Stir in the rice and
cook until rice is heated through.

Scrappy Meal #3
Makes 4 to 6 servings

Time to clean out your fridge again! Find your stray veggies or lonely cans of beans from your pantry.

6 to 8 cups vegan vegetable broth
2 to 3 cups vegetables, diced, i.e., potatoes, carrots, celery
½ cup frozen vegetables, i.e., lima beans, corn, green beans
1 (15 oz.) can of beans
1 tsp. seasoning of choice, i.e., basil, curry, oregano
1 cup sauce, i.e., spaghetti sauce, canned coconut milk, salsa
1 to 2 cups leftover grains, cooked, i.e., rice, quinoa, barley

Place all ingredients except the grain in a medium saucepan and bring to a boil. Reduce heat to medium-low and cook uncovered for 10 to 15 minutes or until vegetables are cooked. Stir in the grain and cook until grain is heated through.

Momma's Dumpling Soup
Makes 4 to 6 servings

We ate dumplings a lot when I was growing up, especially after Thanksgiving. I decided to create a soup around them.

2 Tbsp. extra-virgin olive oil
2 large carrots, thinly sliced
3 stalks celery, thinly sliced
6 cups vegan vegetable broth
1 (15 oz.) can or 1 ½ cups cooked chickpeas, drained and rinsed
1 (15 oz.) can or 1 ½ cups cooked green lentils, drained and rinsed

Dumplings
1 cup whole wheat flour
1 ½ tsp. baking powder
½ tsp. sea salt
1 Tbsp. Earth Balance® Natural Buttery Spread
½ cup non-dairy milk

In a large saucepan, heat oil over medium-high heat and then add carrots and celery, sauté for 3 minutes. Add broth, chickpeas and lentils and bring to a boil, uncovered. Meanwhile, in a small bowl sift together flour, baking soda and salt. Cut in the butter until the mixture is sand-like. Add milk and gently mix until a soft dough forms. With a spoon, drop small dumplings into the boiling soup. Cover tightly and cook uninterrupted for 12 minutes.

Italian Sausage Soup
Makes 6 servings

'Souper' goodness! If you own a pressure cooker, place all ingredients, except the chickpeas and the spinach, in the cooker. Bring up to pressure, reduce heat and then cook for 9 minutes. Remove from heat and allow pressure to drop on its own. After pressure drops, open cooker and then mix in the chickpeas and spinach.

1 Tbsp. extra-virgin olive oil
4 Field Roast® Italian Sausages, casings removed and finely diced
1 medium onion, diced
4 garlic cloves, minced
10 cups vegan vegetable broth
¾ cup barley, soaked in 2 cups water for one hour, then drained
1 cup green lentils, picked over and rinsed
2 Tbsp. dried parsley
1 (15 oz.) can or 1 ½ cups cooked chickpeas, drained and rinsed
1 (16 oz.) bag fresh spinach leaves, chopped
Sea salt, to taste

In a large pot, heat oil over medium-high heat and then add sausages and sauté until browned. Add onion and garlic and sauté until onions are translucent, about 5 minutes. Add broth, barley, lentils and parsley. Bring to a boil and then reduce heat to medium-low, cover and simmer for 35 minutes, or until lentils and barley are cooked. Add chickpeas and spinach, then cook for 5 minutes or until chickpeas are heated through. Season, as needed, with salt.

Whole Wheat Irish Soda Bread
Makes 1 loaf

This makes a great companion to soup. Also, nothing hits the spot like freshly baked bread with vegan butter or some jelly as an afternoon snack. Great for dunking, too.

3 cups whole wheat flour
1 Tbsp. baking powder
$^1/_3$ cup evaporated cane juice
1 tsp. sea salt
1 tsp. baking soda
2 Tbsp. flax seeds, finely ground, mixed with 3 Tbsp. water
2 cups non-dairy milk mixed with 1 Tbsp. apple cider vinegar
¼ cup Earth Balance® Natural Buttery Spread, melted

Preheat oven to 325°F (163°C). Lightly grease a 9 x 5-inch loaf pan with extra-virgin olive oil. Combine flour, baking powder, evaporated cane juice, salt and baking soda. In a small bowl, combine the flax and milk mixtures, then pour into flour mixture. Stir to combine. Add the melted butter and lightly stir until well combined. Pour into greased loaf pan. Bake for 65 to 70 minutes or until toothpick comes out clean. Cool on a wire rack.

Sweet Cornbread
Makes 1 loaf

The mashed banana and cooked sweet potato give this cornbread a moist finish. Prepare to fight at the dinner table to get a piece! Great for dunking, too.

1 cup whole wheat flour
1 tsp. baking powder
½ tsp. baking soda
½ tsp. sea salt
⅛ tsp. allspice
½ cup stone-ground yellow cornmeal
1 cup sweet potato, cooked and mashed
¼ cup extra-virgin olive oil or white bean puree (see page 11)
¼ cup evaporated cane juice
1 medium banana, mashed
½ cup non-dairy milk mixed with 1½ tsp. apple cider vinegar

Preheat oven to 375°F (191 °C). Lightly grease a 9 x 9-inch square baking dish with extra-virgin olive oil. In a medium bowl, add the flour, baking powder, baking soda, salt, allspice and cornmeal. Stir to combine. Add the sweet potato, oil or white bean puree, evaporated cane juice, banana and milk mixture. Gently mix until well incorporated. Pour batter into greased pan and bake for 30 minutes or until a toothpick comes out clean.

Sweet Tooths Anonymous

Cookie Truffles
Makes about 3 dozen truffles

Brace yourselves! These little things are too good to be true. Extra bonus: there may be a few extra cookies to snack on as you make these. Melt the chocolate chips after you chill the truffles for 30 minutes.

2 (13 oz.) packages Newman's Own® Original Crème Filled Chocolate Cookies
1 (8 oz.) tub Follow Your Heart® Vegan Gourmet Cream Cheese or another non-GMO vegan cream cheese, softened
12 oz. semi-sweet vegan chocolate chips, melted

In a food processor, crush 36 cookies into fine crumbs and then place in a medium bowl. Add cream cheese and mix until well incorporated. Roll cookie mixture into 1-inch balls and place on a cookie sheet lined with plant-based wax paper. Chill for 30 minutes. Crush an additional 14 cookies into fine crumbs then place in a small bowl. Dip balls halfway into melted chocolate and then press into reserved cookie crumbs. Return truffles to cookie sheet, crumb side up. Chill an additional 60 minutes.

All-Star Ice Cream Fudge
Makes 48 pieces or more, depending on size

All you could ever want in fudge is right here. Due to the rich taste, make sure to cut these bad boys into small squares. If you're a little nutty, toss some finely chopped raw walnuts into the batter after it has melted. We love to use So Delicious® Dairy Free Coconut Milk Ice Cream, Vanilla Bean flavor. If you are having trouble lifting the fudge out of the dish, simply flip the dish over and run warm water over the bottom for 30-60 seconds. Flip back over and lift out. Repeat as needed. Serve with fresh strawberries on the side.

1 pint container non-dairy vanilla ice cream
40 oz. semi-sweet vegan chocolate chips
1 tsp. vanilla extract

In a large saucepan on medium heat, begin to melt ice cream and then add the chocolate chips, stirring constantly to prevent burning. Once completely melted, remove from heat and stir in vanilla extract. Pour into a 9 x 13-inch baking dish lined with plant-based wax paper. Chill for one hour or until fudge sets. Lift out of dish (see note above) and then cut with a large knife into 1-inch squares.

Mango Raspberry Sorbet
Makes 4 servings

Here is an easy treat for those hot summer days. This also works well poured into Popsicle molds placed in the freezer for at least five hours.

1 (10 oz.) package frozen diced mango
¼ cup frozen raspberries
1 cup water
$^1/_3$ cup agave nectar

Place all ingredients in a high-speed blender and blend until smooth. Pour into a plastic container with a lid. Place in the freezer for two hours or until frozen. Thaw for 5 to10 minutes and then enjoy.

Vanilla Milkshake
Makes 2 servings

Treat yourself to one, you know you want to.

1 pint container So Delicious® Dairy Free Coconut Milk Ice Cream, Vanilla Bean
¾ cup non-dairy milk
¼ tsp. vanilla extract

Place all ingredients in a high-speed blender. Blend until smooth. Serve immediately.

Chocolate Banana Popsicles
Makes 6 or more popsicles

I went on-line and ordered BPA-free Popsicle molds, because I'm weird like that.

1 recipe Chocolate Banana Shake (see page 24)

Pour shake mixture into Popsicle molds. Place in the freezer overnight and enjoy the next day.

Date Tried: _____   Winner: Yes ___ No ___

Ginger Spice and Everything Nice Cookies
Makes about 2 dozen cookies

I adapted these from my Grandma's ginger snap cookies. I loved her cookies.

2 cups whole wheat flour
¾ cup evaporated cane juice
½ tsp. sea salt
2 tsp. baking soda
1 tsp. ground cinnamon
1 tsp. ground cloves
1 tsp. ground ginger
½ medium banana, mashed
$2/_3$ cup unsweetened applesauce
¼ cup molasses

Preheat oven to 350° F (177°C). In a large bowl, combine flour, evaporated cane juice, salt, baking soda, cinnamon, cloves and ginger. In a separate bowl, combine banana, applesauce and molasses. Pour the applesauce mixture into the flour mixture and mix until well incorporated. With a spoon, drop batter onto a cookie sheet lightly greased with extra-virgin olive oil. Bake for 10 to 12 minutes.

Party Time

Beverage-Worthy Salsa
Makes approximately 12 cups

I provided food for my sister's voice recital receptions. At her first recital one of her classmates of Hispanic descent asked for the leftover salsa at the end of the night. She later confessed that she drank the salsa on her way home. If you can't find El Pato® Jalapeño Salsa, omit it and replace two of the diced tomato cans with diced tomatoes with jalapeños.

3 (28 oz.) cans diced tomatoes
2 bunches green onions, diced
1 bunch fresh cilantro, leaves only
1 (7.75 oz.) can El Pato® Jalapeño Salsa
½ cup canned green chiles, diced
1 jalapeño pepper, diced
1 Tbsp. sea salt
1 Tbsp. onion powder
1 Tbsp. garlic powder
1½ tsp. cumin

Combine all ingredients in a very large bowl. Stir until well combined. In batches, pulse salsa in a blender and transfer to containers with lids, i.e., mason jars, plastic containers.

Easy Breezy Guacamole
Makes 4 servings

When I was raw vegan I made this and ate it with celery sticks and raw crackers.

2 avocadoes, pitted and mashed
4 stalks green onions, diced
¼ tsp. sea salt, or to taste
½ tsp. lemon juice, or to taste

In a small bowl, add all ingredients and mix well. Serve immediately.

Cowboy Caviar
Makes 12 servings

Giddy up!

1 (15 oz.) can black-eyed peas, drained and rinsed
1 (15 oz.) can black beans, drained and rinsed
1 (15 oz.) can organic corn, drained and rinsed
2 cups tomatoes, diced
1 (0.7 oz.) packet dry Italian dressing mix
¼ cup canned green chiles, diced
1 bunch green onions, diced
Lime juice, to taste
Garlic salt, to taste
Sea salt, to taste
6 avocados, pitted and diced

In a large bowl, add all the ingredients except the avocados. Mix well to combine. Gently fold in avocados. Cover and chill for 30 minutes to meld flavors. Serve with tortilla chips.

3-2-1 Dip
Makes 4 servings

I had a version of this at a birthday party when I was in elementary school. I liked it then and I like the vegan version now.

1 (8 oz.) tub Follow Your Heart® Vegan Gourmet Cream Cheese or another non-GMO vegan cream cheese, softened
2 cups Beverage-Worthy Salsa (see page 101) or 1 (16 oz.) jar of store-bought salsa
½ cup Daiya® cheddar style shreds, or more to taste

Preheat oven to 350°F (177°C). Spread cream cheese on the bottom of a 9 x 13- inch baking dish. Pour salsa over top and spread evenly. Sprinkle cheese on top and bake for 30 minutes.   Serve with tortilla chips.

Sneaky Chocolate-Peanut Squares
Makes about 10 cups

This is a less-sweet version of the traditional chocolate-peanut squares treat. I replace the powdered sugar with arrowroot starch and stevia. I feel like a mad scientist when I whisk the two ingredients together as it can create a cloud of 'smoke.' If you are a sugar addict and need the sweeter version, simply grind evaporated cane juice in a coffee grinder to make a quick powdered sugar equaling 1 ½ cups. Many refined sugars and powdered sugars are processed using animal bones which is a vegan no-no. Several of my omnivore taste-testers for this recipe were two to eight years old. They all asked for more.

8 cups crunchy rice squares cereal
½ cup peanuts, roasted and salted
$^1/_3$ cup raisins
$^2/_3$ cup non-hydrogenated peanut butter
1 cup semi-sweet vegan chocolate chips
1 ½ cups arrowroot starch
3 packets Sweetleaf Stevia® Sweetener

In a large bowl, combine the cereal, peanuts and raisins, set aside. In a small saucepan over medium-low heat, melt the peanut butter and chocolate chips until smooth, stirring constantly. Pour chocolate mixture onto cereal mixture and stir until all pieces are evenly coated. In a small bowl, combine arrowroot and stevia and whisk until well combined. Place arrowroot mixture in a large re-sealable plastic bag. Add the cereal mixture, seal securely and shake the bag until all pieces are evenly coated. Chill for 20 minutes.

Beet-aful Chocolate Cake
Makes one 9 x 13-inch cake

No one detected the beets in this cake. (Insert evil laugh here). Because of the whole wheat flour, it will be denser than typical cakes. I like to use fresh raspberries mashed and sweetened with agave nectar, instead of traditional frosting, to drizzle on top of the cake. To make beet puree, use freshly cooked or canned beets, drained, and pureed with ¼ cup of water in a food processor.

1 cup beet puree (see note above)
1 cup unsweetened applesauce
$^1/_8$ cup water
1 tsp. vanilla extract
1 tsp. apple cider vinegar
1½ cups whole wheat flour
½ cup cacao or cocoa powder
1 cup evaporated cane juice
1 Tbsp. cornstarch
2 tsp. baking soda
½ tsp. sea salt
¼ tsp. ground cinnamon

Preheat oven to 325°F (163°C). Lightly grease a 9 x 13-inch baking dish with extra-virgin olive oil. In a small bowl, add beet puree, applesauce, water, vanilla and vinegar; mix well. In a large bowl, add flour, cacao or cocoa, evaporated cane juice, cornstarch, baking soda, salt and cinnamon; mix well. Add the beet mixture to the flour mixture and stir until well combined. Pour into greased 9 x 13-inch baking dish and bake for 35 minutes or until a toothpick comes out clean.

First Birthday Cake
Makes one 9 x 13-inch cake

The idea of a traditional birthday cake with frosting for any of my little kids makes me cringe. Here is another option minus the sugar rush. Again, because of the whole wheat flour, it is denser than a traditional cake. For the frosting, simply put plain non-dairy yogurt in a small bowl and mix it with a few frozen blueberries for blue or frozen cherries for red. Mash the fruit for a more intense color. Remove the fruit and place the yogurt frosting on top of the cutie's slice.

2 cups whole wheat flour
1 Tbsp. flax seeds, finely ground
1 tsp. baking soda
6 ripe medium bananas, mashed
1 cup unsweetened applesauce
$^1/_3$ cup non-dairy milk

Preheat oven to 325°F (163°C). Lightly grease a 9 x 13-inch baking dish with extra-virgin olive oil, set aside. In a large bowl, combine the flour, flax seeds and baking soda, set aside. In a medium bowl, combine bananas, applesauce and milk. Pour the banana mixture into the flour mixture and stir until well incorporated. Pour batter into greased baking dish and bake for 90 minutes or until a sharp knife inserted in the middle of cake comes out clean.

More Party Ideas

Mini-Marry Me Muffins (see page 29): Pour the batter into a lined mini-cupcake pan and bake for 15 minutes at 400°F (204°C).

Fresh organic fruit and berries: Don't underestimate them, especially the berries.

White Bean Hummus (see page 39): Serve with fresh veggies.

Hummus and Veggie Pinwheels: Take whole grain or sprouted tortillas and spread with the desired amount of White Bean Hummus (see page 39), approximately 2 to 4 Tbsp. per tortilla. Don't spread the hummus all the way to the edge. If you're feeling spunky, add a few dashes of your favorite hot sauce. Then on top of the hummus arrange any of your favorite toppings, i.e., shredded carrots, thinly sliced cucumber, thinly sliced avocado, spinach leaves or thinly sliced tomatoes. Gently roll up the tortillas and then cut 1-inch segments to create the pinwheels. Secure with toothpicks as needed.

Kettle Brand Tias!™ Salsa Picante tortilla chips

Fresh Juice

Juice Fasting

Although we juice several times a week, I wasn't anticipating adding a mini-chapter on juicing recipes. But, as I was compiling this book, I ran into some health issues and turned to juice fasting to cleanse my body. I feel so much better now and it would be silly of me not to include a small section on juicing.

By any stretch of the imagination, I am not an expert on juice fasting. I do know through what little experience I do have that it is tremendously healing, energizing and beneficial. The books that I turned to during my first juice fast were *The Juice Fasting Bible: Discover the Power of All-Juice Diets to Restore Good Health, Lose Weight and Increase Vitality* by Dr. Sandra Cabot and *The New Life Fasting Guide: Seven Days to a Healthier, Happier You* by Hellmut Lützner, M.D. In preparing for additional fasts, I've also enjoyed *The Transformational Power of Fasting: The Way to Spiritual, Physical, and Emotional Rejuvenation* by Stephen Harrod Buhner.

There are countless ways to combine and juice greens, fruits and vegetables. I will share a few examples and a few lists of what our favorites are in the next few pages.

Pineapple Paradise
Makes 2 servings

This is a multi-flavored treat.

2 spears pineapple
5 medium carrots
2 apples, cored
1 bunch spinach
1 handful fresh basil leaves (stems included)
1-inch fresh ginger
½ to 1 lime, peeled
Water (optional)

Run all ingredients through a juicer. Add water to dilute as desired.

Super Green
Makes 2 servings

The quantity of greens in this recipe packs a nutritional punch. If you need to add more apples, don't be ashamed! Initially, we used a lot of apples.

1 bunch kale
1 bunch spinach
½ bunch dandelion leaves
4 stalks celery
1 cucumber
5 to 7 apples, cored, or more to taste
1-inch fresh ginger
½ lemon, peeled
Water (optional)

Run all ingredients through a juicer. Add water to dilute as desired.

Again, if you aren't used to greens, there is no harm in juicing more apples to make it more palatable. If money is tight, substitute store-bought 100% organic apple juice for the apples, and add to the juiced greens mixture until it is palatable. Over time you will find you won't need to sweeten it up as much, thus saving more money.

Elixir of Love
Makes 1 to 2 servings

This green juice is my husband's favorite. Whenever he is in need of a surprise at work, I'll whip up a batch. I love seeing his reaction when his eye catches the juice-filled mason jar. Sometimes, he'll even squeal out a "yes!" like a five-year old. Too cute!

1 bunch kale
3 to 6 apples
1 cucumber
½ lemon, peeled
Water (optional)

Run all ingredients through a juicer. Add water to dilute as desired.

Morning Pick-Me-Up
Makes 2 servings

Sweet and spicy based on how much ginger you use. Since I choose not to drink coffee, tea or soda this is a great energizer for me.

3 oranges, peeled
5 carrots
1 medium beet
$^1/_2$ to 1-inch fresh ginger
Water (optional)

Run all ingredients through a juicer. Add water to dilute as desired.

Juicing tips

Favorite greens are bok choy, dandelion leaves (very bitter so combine with another green), kale, spinach (bunches, not the bagged leaves), Swiss chard and wheat grass.

Favorite sweeteners are apples, butternut squash, carrots, oranges, pears and pineapple.

Other regular ingredients include beets (in small amounts), celery, cucumber, ginger and lemons.

Occasionally used ingredients include basil, broccoli, cauliflower, cilantro, eggplant, grapefruit, limes, parsley, radishes, sweet potatoes, tomatoes and turnips.

Single ingredient juices
Heirloom tomatoes (with a dash of sea salt mixed in)
Watermelon (add some jalapeño for a spicy kick)

Resources I Rely On and Recommend

Books

Buhner, Stephen Harrod. *The Transformational Power of Fasting: The Way to Spiritual, Physical, and Emotional Rejuvenation.* Rochester, VT: Healing Arts Press. 2012.

*Cabot, Sandra. *The Juice Fasting Bible: Discover the Power of All-Juice Diets to Restore Good Health, Lose Weight and Increase Vitality.* Berkeley, CA: Ulysses Press, 2007.

*Campbell, T. Colin, and Thomas M. Campbell II. *The China Study: The Most Comprehensive Study of Nutrition Ever Conducted and the Startling Implications for Diet, Weight Loss, and Long-Term Health.* Dallas, TX: Benbella Books, 2006.

Campbell, T. Colin, and Howard Jacobson. *Whole: Rethinking the Science of Nutrition.* Dallas, TX: Benbella Books, 2013.

Cousens, Gabriel. *Conscious Eating.* Berkeley, CA: North Atlantic Books, 2000.

_____. *Rainbow Green Life-Food Cuisine.* Berkeley, CA: North Atlantic Books, 2003.

Esselstyn, Caldwell. *Prevent and Reverse Heart Disease.* New York: Avery Publishing, 2007.

Kordich, Jay. *The Juiceman®'s Power of Juicing: Delicious Juice Recipes for Energy, Health, Weight Loss, and Relief from Scores of Common Ailments.* New York, NY: William Morrow and Company, Inc., 1992.

Lützner, Hellmut. *The New Life Fasting Guide: Seven Days to a Healthier, Happier You.* New York, NY: The Crossroad Publishing Company, 2012.

*Robbins, John. *Diet for a New America.* Tiburon, CA: H J Kramer, 1987.

_____. *Healthy at 100.* New York: Random House, 2006.

*_____. *Reclaiming Our Health: Exploding the Medical Myth and Embracing the Source of True Healing.* Tiburon, CA: H J Kramer, 1996.

*_____. *The Food Revolution: How Your Diet Can Help Save Your Life and Our World.* York Beach, ME: Conari Press, 2001.

Videos

Fat, Sick and Nearly Dead. Directed by Joe Cross, Kurt Engfehr. 2010. El Segundo, CA: Gravitas Ventures, 2011, video and VOD.

Forks Over Knives. Directed by Lee Fulkerson. 2011. New York, NY: Virgil Films & Entertainment, 2011, video.

Website

*www.happycow.net My go-to website for finding vegan-friendly restaurants and grocery stores. This is a must-use resource for planning Quamo road trips!

*highly recommended

Index

About the Author

Jaclyn Quamo was born in the Finger Lakes area of upstate New York. She loved watching her Nonnie cook and enjoyed eating her food. Since she was young, music and food have been a big part of her life. She attended SUNY Fredonia where she earned her bachelor's degree in music education. During her college years, she realized how much she loved to cook and feed her family, friends and the missionaries of The Church of Jesus Christ of Latter-Day Saints. Upon graduating from SUNY Fredonia, she and her new husband Jeff moved to Arizona to earn degrees in clarinet performance at Arizona State University. Jaclyn is now in her tenth year as a public school music and band teacher. She enjoys teaching, performing and cooking. Having a natural curiosity, a desire to learn and a love for food has helped her to develop her talents in the kitchen. In her spare time, she loves to be with family and friends watching movies, playing games and being outdoors. She loves being a thrifty shopper. She is passionate about learning new things and always aspires to become a better person.

See www.mormon.org to find, as did Jaclyn, the source of true happiness, our purpose in life and the greatest love of all.

"Perhaps the greatest charity comes when we are kind to each other, when we don't judge or categorize someone else, when we simply give each other the benefit of the doubt or remain quiet. Charity is accepting someone's differences, weaknesses, and shortcomings; having patience with someone who has let us down; or resisting the impulse to become offended when someone doesn't handle something the way we might have hoped. Charity is refusing to take advantage of another's weakness and being willing to forgive someone who has hurt us. Charity is expecting the best of each other." -Marvin J. Ashton

Made in the USA
San Bernardino, CA
15 March 2014